The New York Times

LOOKING FORWARD

Crowdfunding

EDUCATIONAL PUBLISHING BOOKS

THE NEW YORK TIMES EDITORIAL STAFF

Published in 2020 by New York Times Educational Publishing
in association with The Rosen Publishing Group, Inc.
29 East 21st Street, New York, NY 10010

First Edition

The New York Times
Alex Ward: Editorial Director, Book Development
Phyllis Collazo: Photo Rights/Permissions Editor
Heidi Giovine: Administrative Manager

Rosen Publishing
Megan Kellerman: Managing Editor
Hanna Washburn: Editor
Greg Tucker: Creative Director
Brian Garvey: Art Director

Cataloging-in-Publication Data
Names: New York Times Company.
Title: Crowdfunding / edited by the New York Times editorial staff.
Description: New York : New York Times Educational Publishing, 2020. | Series: Looking forward | Includes glossary and index.
Identifiers: ISBN 9781642822571 (library bound) | ISBN 9781642822564 (pbk.) | ISBN 9781642822588 (ebook)
Subjects: LCSH: Crowd funding—Juvenile literature. | Electronic fund raising—Juvenile literature. | Venture capital—Juvenile literature.
Classification: LCC HG4751.C769 2020 | DDC 658.15'224—dc23

Manufactured in the United States of America

On the cover: What started as a handful of websites promoting people's pet projects has transformed into hundreds of platforms that serve as vehicles for not only fund-raising but also product development and market research; Minh Uong/The New York Times.

Contents

CHAPTER 2

Supporting the Arts and Entertainment

Introduction

IN THE AGE of social sharing and personal networks, a new form of fund-raising has gained significant traction. Whether you are a paleontologist seeking financial assistance for fossil excavation or a musician looking to fund your first album, people are turning to crowdfunding as a way to realize projects, spread awareness about a cause and even cover medical expenses. Although community-based fund-raising has been around for centuries, crowdfunding refers specifically to funds generated through the Internet. The current model typically involves three parties: the person or group who proposes the project, the community of people that support the venture and the platform that mediates the exchange. Some of the most popular platforms include GoFundMe, Indiegogo, Kickstarter and Patreon.

This method of fund-raising can allow otherwise unfeasible projects to be realized, and allows for a large community of people to be involved and contribute what they can to a cause. This allows for a level of audience engagement that generates enthusiasm for the project and can create a dedicated fan base. Creators will often share updates with their funders, who in turn can provide feedback, allowing for a reciprocal relationship rarely found in other kinds of fund-raising.

Crowdfunding also offers numerous benefits to the project producers beyond financial gain. In addition to generating income, a compelling project can also boost the reputation of the initiators. Even if the fund-raising is unsuccessful, the venture can give them a sense of their audience and the market for their idea. They can even opt to provide pre-release access to content or the opportunity for beta-testing to their funders. Crowdfunding is an especially appealing method

JAKE NAUGHTON FOR THE NEW YORK TIMES

Offices for Kickstarter, the popular online crowdfunding website, at their headquarters in New York, Sept. 15, 2015.

for unconventional projects that might not fit the mold for traditional financiers but can gain traction to generate support across a wide range of diverse and enthusiastic people.

Crowdfunding has been utilized for a wide variety of entrepreneurial projects, and this volume designates four major areas where it has been most prominent. Scientists, researchers and entrepreneurs have used crowdfunding, especially if they have been unsuccessful trying to obtain funds through traditional methods such as foundation grants. Community-sourced funds have been used to produce smart watches, conduct research on lake pollution and build bionic pancreases. Arts and entertainment projects are also common, including the famous example of the fan-backed "Veronica Mars" reunion film, which broke several fund-raising records in 2012 and demonstrated the power of passionate fans in a crowdfunding context. Even political activism and philanthropy endeavors have benefited from crowdfunding, raising funds for refugees and victims of natural disasters or mass shootings.

Gaining traction and controversy in more recent years are personal crowdfunding campaigns. Asking for support from the community to cover medical care, a memorial service, education expenses or even a much-needed vacation has become increasingly common. Crowdfunding as a tool can create a casual and accessible environment where people in need feel they can ask, and those that can help may do so. The lack of accountability and relative anonymity of those asking for help, however, means the funds generated for a certain cause may in fact be used for something else, or even the heartwarming story used as an appeal could be false.

This is one major way that crowdfunding attracts controversy, but it is not the only one. Celebrities like Zach Braff and Spike Lee have attracted debate when asking for help funding their projects, as many consider it in poor taste for the rich and famous to solicit funds from the crowd. Established celebrities likely have access to more traditional forms of financing, and their presence on platforms like Kickstarter can take space and attention away from first-time project producers in more dire need. Their presence on these sites, however, can widen the donor pool, and may encourage people to patronize other crowdfunded projects.

The rapid rise of crowdfunding is a complex issue, and it is undeniable that many innovations we enjoy today would not exist without this method of fund-raising. As social media and networking continue to be omnipresent in contemporary culture, it is clear that crowdfunding is here to stay, though its structure will likely change and adapt alongside innovations in science, technology, the arts and activism.

CHAPTER 1

Funding Science, Technology and Start-Up Companies

In recent years, scientists, researchers and entrepreneurs have turned to crowdfunding to get their projects off the ground, especially when traditional methods of financing have been unsuccessful. In 2016, a new rule was established allowing anyone to risk $2,000 a year or more investing in small companies in exchange for a stake in the business. This ruling represents a major shift toward accessible investing for a more diverse group — not just the wealthy — fueling a greater range of crowdfunded research and products. This chapter details a variety of crowdfunded ventures in the realms of science, technology and emerging companies from 2012 through 2017.

Young Scientists Embrace Crowdfunding

BY KELLY SLIVKA | MAY 29, 2012

CROWDFUNDING, OR APPEALING to the online community for funds for personal projects, seems to be thriving. One of the best-known platforms is Kickstarter, which generally features projects that are creative in nature — musicians seeking to record an album, for example, or inventors pursuing an idea.

But young scientists struggling unsuccessfully to obtain funds through traditional routes like foundation grants are also experimenting with crowdfunding these days. Among them is Mary Rogalski, a doctoral candidate in forestry and environmental studies at Yale who hopes to crowdfund some of her research for her thesis on lake pollution. She turned to #SciFund Challenge, a fund-raising campaign tailored for scientists.

"I didn't really know what I was getting into, so I didn't have high expectations," said Ms. Rogalski, one of 75 scientists hoping to meet their fund-raising goals in the current round of the #SciFund Challenge, which ends on Thursday.

"I have had sort of a dry spell in terms of grant writing," Ms. Rogalski said.

She knew that a couple of other students in her lab had tried crowdfunding projects, so she decided to give it a whirl. "It's this weird, fluid time where people are experimenting with new things to see what the possibilities are," she said.

Inspired by Kickstarter's success, two ecologists at the University of California, Santa Barbara, Jai Ranganathan and Jarrett Byrnes, opened the first round of the #SciFund Challenge last year. Dr. Byrnes said he and Dr. Ranganathan saw it as an opportunity to persuade scientists to engage the public.

"There's very little incentive for scientists to do anything other than their research," said Dr. Byrnes, referring to the publish-or-perish culture of academia, in which scientists' success is measured by publication in peer-reviewed research journals.

Any interested scientist with a feasible project and a fund-raising goal can sign up for the challenge, Dr. Byrnes said. In the month before the challenge begins, each entrant receives instruction in how to make an engaging video about his or her project to be posted on Rockethub.com, a crowdfunding platform that hosts the #SciFund Challenge.

The scientists are then given an opportunity to share and critique the videos with one another before they go live. "It's a community process," Dr. Byrnes said.

In the first challenge, which ran from Nov. 1 to Dec. 15, 49 scientists took part, raising $76,230 altogether. The current challenge has raised just under $84,000 in 28 days, with 22 of the 75 scientists meeting their goals so far.

Ms. Rogalski has raised $2,026, just over her initial goal of $2,000, and has enjoyed the experience. "It's not just a way to make money — it's a bigger thing than that," she said.

Challenge participants are encouraged to keep their donors involved as the research progresses, fostering a long-term relationship with a supportive public. "Reaching out to people and having people respond has been really positive," she said.

More seasoned scientists are also excited about the potential of crowdfunding. "I think we're going to see this really, really take off," said Ms. Rogalski's adviser, David Skelly, the associate dean for research at Yale's School of Forestry and Environmental Studies.

First, people can now easily educate themselves about scientific fields that interest them and have a voice in what they would like to see financed, he said. Second, federal research grants are harder and harder to come by.

"You have more people asking for more money and a diminished availability of funds," said Dr. Skelly, adding that the percentage of applicants receiving National Science Foundation awards had been steadily declining. The upshot is that scientists have to cast a wider net.

Crowdfunding has drawn its share of criticism. Some argue that it is biased in favor of trendy projects (people are more likely to support polar bear research than cyanobacteria research) and that the projects seeking funds have not been peer-reviewed. (At the National Science Foundation, scientists review the proposals of other scientists to judge the worthiness of their research proposals.)

But in Dr. Skelly's view, the benefits seem to trump the drawbacks. "For the first time in my career — and I got my Ph.D. 20 years ago — there's a dialogue going on between scientists doing primary research and the public," he said.

That is what Dr. Byrnes and Dr. Ranganathan say they were hoping for. Dr. Byrnes said his passion for science communication was driven largely by his main areas of study, climate change and human-caused extinctions of species. He argues that people should have access to the best knowledge possible about the world they live in.

"I want the information that people have when they make decisions about their lives, about policy, and about how they raise their voices, to be informed by solid, accurate science," he said.

Dr. Byrnes said he and Dr. Ranganathan were not sure what the future held for the #SciFund Challenge, but that they hoped to increase the scope of its fund-raising.

Pebble Raises $15 Million as Wave of Smart Watches Arrives

BY JENNA WORTHAM | MAY 16, 2013

RUMOR HAS IT that everyone from Apple to Microsoft is working on smartwatches to compete with the handful that are already arriving on the market.

But before those started making waves, there was the Pebble, a Kickstarter project begun last April in order to build a durable sports watch that could also receive text messages and calls and play music. Before anyone had seen a finished product, it dazzled tens of thousands of people online, who then contributed $10 million to see the device manufactured.

And on Thursday, Pebble announced it had raised $15 million from Charles River Ventures to propel the company out of its idea phase and into full-on start-up mode.

Eric Migicovsky, the Canadian engineer who started the Pebble project, said that it had already shipped 70,000 watches to its Kickstarter backers; it owes them another 15,000, which it is rushing out. The company is also planning to sell watches through its site. He said that if Pebble wants to continue to work on future designs, it will need additional financial support and advisement.

"When we started shipping Pebble at the end of January, we realized that if we were looking at a larger opportunity than we originally anticipated, we might need more support, a larger network and some capital to pull it off," he said. Pebble spent most of its original $10 million on manufacturing.

Mr. Migicovsky said his primary plans are to support the growing community of developers who have already built 600 apps for the Pebble smartwatch. He said that there is a message board on Reddit, a news aggregator, dedicated to Pebble add-ons and products, including a shower holster that lets owners mount their watches while they bathe.

In addition, he said, he wants to hire more software developers and people who can start prototyping what the second-generation Pebble smartwatches might look like. Both of these things will help safeguard Pebble from the onslaught of competition likely to come from industry heavyweights like Google, Apple, Samsung and Microsoft.

"Obviously others have recognized the opportunity," he said. "But we're going to focus on what we're good at, which is building a sports watch with a long battery life that looks good."

Pebble is not the only Kickstarter project that sought outside funds after an initial whirlwind of crowdfunded support. Ouya, an Android-based gaming console, also recently announced that it had raised $15 million in venture financing.

Crowdfunding Site CircleUp Raises $14 Million

BY WILLIAM ALDEN | MARCH 26, 2014

CIRCLEUP, A CROWDFUNDING WEBSITE, has allowed a number of fledgling companies to raise money over the last two years. Now, CircleUp has attracted some additional money of its own.

The start-up announced on Wednesday that it had raised $14 million in a financing round led by Canaan Partners, a venture capital firm investing in the company for the first time. Previous investors, including Google Ventures and Union Square Ventures, participated in the round.

The fresh capital underscores the excitement in Silicon Valley over new ways of raising money. Crowdfunding, in particular, has drawn interest, and other platforms, like AngelList, have also attracted millions in venture capital. Crowdfunding was made easier in 2012 by the Jumpstart Our Business Startups Act, or JOBS Act.

CircleUp offers investors equity in small consumer and retail companies, which are vetted to weed out potential duds. Prospective investors — provided they are "accredited," meaning they make at least $200,000 a year or have a net worth above $1 million — can read about the companies on the CircleUp site and invest through the platform. CircleUp collects a commission from the companies.

The companies that have used the site to raise money include Madécasse, a Brooklyn-based chocolate maker, and Ocean's Halo, a maker of seaweed chips. CircleUp says it has helped more than 30 companies raise over $30 million since the platform opened in April 2012.

Ryan Caldbeck, chief executive and co-founder of CircleUp, claimed that the company, which raised $7.5 million last year, did not need the additional money. But he said he embraced the opportunity to work with Dan Ciporin, a partner at Canaan Partners, who is joining CircleUp's board.

The addition of Mr. Ciporin, who is also on the board of Lending Club, a fast-growing company that connects borrowers to lenders online, and which is aiming to go public this year, offers a clue to CircleUp's ambitions.

"There's a lot that we can learn from Dan's experience at Lending Club," Mr. Caldbeck, who formerly worked in private equity, said in an interview. "We viewed that as a really good analogy of what we're trying to build."

Crowdfunding Tips for Turning Inspiration Into Reality

BY KATE MURPHY | JAN. 22, 2014

MIKE WHITEHEAD'S BIG IDEA was to design a better cast-iron skillet. Stephanie Turenko's big idea was to make an animated short film about her Ukrainian grandmother. Colin Owen's big idea was to manufacture a hard-to-steal bike light.

Many of us have ideas like that, hatched while staring out the window or doodling on a cocktail napkin. And that's where the dream ends, stunted by a lack of capital, credibility and confidence.

Not anymore. Online crowdfunding is helping better cast-iron skillets and other big ideas become reality.

What started as a handful of websites promoting people's pet projects has turned into hundreds of platforms that serve as vehicles for not only fund-raising — the record is $10.2 million — but also product development and market research.

But succeeding at crowdfunding isn't as easy as raising your hand and saying you need money. It demands strategy and stamina, though a sincere appeal can still trump the slickest competitor.

"A lot of people think if they just put their project on Kickstarter, money will start rolling in," said Mr. Whitehead, who used the popular Kickstarter crowdfunding platform last fall to raise $211,027. "It's not as easy as it looks."

Successful crowdfunding campaigns, most often 30 days long, take several months of preparation. With the help of an industrial designer, Mr. Whitehead first spent six months developing a prototype skillet in his Portland, Ore., basement so he'd have something to show potential backers. He then spent another four months reaching out to friends and family as well as culinary, technology and design publications, alerting them to his coming Kickstarter campaign.

While Kickstarter is to crowdfunding what Kleenex is to tissues, there are many other highly trafficked sites that perform similar functions, like Indiegogo, RocketHub and Crowdtilt. There are also niche sites like PubSlush, which caters to aspiring authors, and Appbackr, which is a home for hopeful app developers. They vary not only in the types of projects presented, but also in their fee structure, geographic coverage and whether you can keep what you raise or lose everything if you don't reach your fund-raising goal.

Ms. Turenko, who is from Toronto but is teaching English in Slovakia, chose RocketHub to raise money for her animated film. "They take a higher percentage if you don't make your goal, but you do get to keep what you raise," she said. That's a big difference from Kickstarter, where you can lose everything if you don't make your goal.

"I'd rather be allowed to take what I can get," Ms. Turenko said. So far, she has raised $4,066 toward a goal of $7,000 with 15 days of fund-raising remaining.

There is also a growing number of private equity crowdfunding websites like Crowdfunder and CircleUp, where investors can buy shares in start-ups rather than just make a donation.

Currently, equity crowdfunding is limited to wealthy, so-called accredited investors. But less moneyed investors will soon get their chance thanks to preliminary guidelines published last year as part of the Jumpstart Our Business Startups, or JOBS, Act.

Regardless of which platform you choose, keep in mind that people don't back projects randomly. "The crowd is quite rational and sensitive to signals of quality," said Ethan Mollick, an assistant professor and crowdfunding researcher at the Wharton School of the University of Pennsylvania.

Many in the crowd are early adopters of technology and enjoy watching as a big idea turns into an actual product that they, as early backers, often receive first as a reward for their donation. Crowdfunding platforms don't like to call this preordering since there are no guarantees, but that's essentially what it is.

"We don't present products that are already completed and sitting on some shelf in Iowa shrink-wrapped and ready to ship," said the Kickstarter co-founder Yancey Strickler. "You actually have a role in something coming to life. You know the creators and see the process from the beginning."

Not surprisingly, a clear and concise presentation of your idea through video, illustrations and text is essential. Put yourself in the place of a would-be funder scrolling through projects. You've got maybe 30 seconds to grab their attention and less than that to turn them off. There is an entire crowdfunding support system of video producers, editors and other consultants listed on sites like CrowdCrux if you need help.

"A single spelling error reduces chances of success by 13 percent," said Mr. Mollick at Wharton. Oddly, his research also indicates that mentioning how nerdy you are, and referring to Star Wars seems to help — a clue to the type of people trolling the more popular crowdfunding sites.

But your audience is also venture capitalists, who view a successful crowdfunding campaign as proof that your big idea is viable and worthy of their attention. Mr. Owen said he didn't consider starting a crowdfunding campaign for his theft-resistant bicycle lights until a venture capitalist said he wouldn't consider investing until he did.

"I felt crowdfunding was like having a bake sale to fund your company," said Mr. Owen, who lives in San Francisco and raised $66,386 on Kickstarter in November. "What I came to realize was it wasn't so much the money as the validation."

With crowd-conveyed credibility, he was able to get a Small Business Administration loan to pay for the first production run of his lights, which 500 people on Kickstarter were promised in exchange for their financial support. Moreover, venture capitalists are now knocking on his door rather than the other way around.

Because he was out to demonstrate demand more than find money, Mr. Owen's crowdfunding goal of $45,000 was based on what similar projects were able to raise rather than what he actually needed to make his product.

Rachel Gant and Andrew Deming, on the other hand, asked the crowd for $20,000 because that was precisely the amount required to manufacture their big idea: tote bags that unzipped into picnic blankets. They raised $25,765 on Kickstarter and now two months later they are shipping totes to their funders as promised.

"We didn't go to a bank because we decided we wanted to build a community around our new company so people would be more interested and invested," said Ms. Gant, who lives in San Francisco. "It was also sort of like research to see how people would react to the product."

She said she got suggestions for colors and also learned the product appealed particularly to mothers with small children who could use it as a toy bag and play mat. "We never would have thought of that because we aren't parents," she said. "If you just got money from a bank you wouldn't have that kind of interaction with people."

Crowdfunding experts and veterans of the process agree that such engagement with potential funders, together with a clear vision and a sincere belief in a product, are hallmarks of successful campaigns. But more than anything, your big idea has to be a good idea.

"If you don't have a good idea, even the slickest crowdfunding campaign won't fly," said Mr. Whitehead, a self-described serial entrepreneur who is currently overseeing the manufacture of the 1,550 iron skillets he presold on Kickstarter. "You can sit through marketing classes, you can get an M.B.A., but put it out there for the crowd and you will learn the physics of bootstrapping real fast."

Start-Ups Turn to the Crowd for Financing

BY SYDNEY EMBER | DEC. 10, 2014

LESLIE LIENAU IS hunting for cash, again.

After raising $41,000 in a Kickstarter campaign last year, she is hoping to expand her company, which makes educational tools for artists. But like many small-business owners, Ms. Lienau, who owns the Conservatory for Classical Art, an art school in Edmond, Okla., says traditional financing is elusive.

Banks will not lend to her. A venture capital investment is out of the question.

"Our company is too new, and our product is not in a place where we can scale fast enough," Ms. Lienau, 53, said in an interview last

NICK OXFORD FOR THE NEW YORK TIMES

Leslie Lienau, owner of Miira Artist Tools in Edmond, Okla., raised financing for her company through a Kickstarter campaign.

month. "It's just so much better for us to bootstrap it, so to speak, and go to the crowd."

Ms. Lienau's company, Miira Artist Tools, is the kind of fledgling company President Obama wanted to help in 2012 when he signed the Jumpstart Our Business Startups Act, better known as the JOBS Act. Part of the law, Title III, was intended to allow small businesses seeking capital to crowdfund, or raise money from virtually anyone, by selling stock and other securities over the Internet. "Start-ups and small business will now have access to a big, new pool of potential investors," Mr. Obama said at the time. "For the first time, ordinary Americans will be able to go online and invest in entrepreneurs that they believe in."

Congress directed the Securities and Exchange Commission to finalize the rules by December 2012, but the agency has yet to do so. As it reviews Title III of the JOBS Act, a debate has raged. Supporters say crowdfunding is an innovative way to finance new ideas. Others say the high risk associated with backing early-stage businesses is inappropriate for ordinary investors.

Only accredited investors — those with annual income of more than $200,000 or $1 million in net worth not including their primary residence — are permitted to participate in crowdfunding deals. Under the proposed rules, which the S.E.C. introduced in October 2013, businesses could raise up to $1 million in a 12-month period without registering the offering with the agency.

"The goal is to democratize and improve finance," said Representative Patrick T. McHenry, Republican of North Carolina, who worked on the House crowdfunding bill that was incorporated into the JOBS Act.

In writing its rules, the S.E.C. adopted strict requirements intended to minimize fraud and protect investors. Individuals who are not accredited investors, for instance, would face limits on how much they could invest. Businesses would be required to go through a registered broker or a new type of registered platform called a funding portal for their offerings. Businesses also would be required to submit audited financial statements. The rules are still under review and may change.

But critics are concerned that the rules do not do enough to protect investors, however sophisticated they may be.

"Without anybody doing anything wrong, without any fraud, most start-ups fail," said Barbara Roper, director of investor protection at the Consumer Federation of America, a nonprofit advocacy group. "We're actually encouraging people to make investments that we would deem to be unsuitable if they were recommended by a broker."

The S.E.C. declined to comment.

Despite the long wait for the rules to be completed, start-ups across the country are expressing interest in crowdfunding. Many see it as a way to form deeper ties with early customers by giving them a stake in the company's success.

Funding platforms have been preparing for what they hope will be enormous demand once the law takes effect.

One platform, Wefunder, has about 34,000 investors and has helped companies — including one that builds flying cars — raise more than $5 million from accredited investors, said Mike Norman, Wefunder's co-founder and president. Dealflicks, a discount site for movie tickets, based in Los Angeles, used Wefunder this year to raise $173,450 from 64 backers.

Another funding platform, SeedInvest, began doing accredited deals about 18 months ago, said Kiran Lingam, general counsel for the company. But he said the excitement about Title III crowdfunding had appeared to wane. "There's sort of a wait-and-see approach," Mr. Lingam said. "Title III is just so far removed because of the delay that it's not really top of mind."

In Indiana, the crowdfunding platform Localstake has used certain securities laws to allow companies to raise money through a process that more closely resembles true crowdfunding. Under one rule, for example, businesses in a state may raise capital from investors in that state.

Through Localstake, Cardinal Spirits, a distillery based in Bloomington, Ind., raised $850,000 last year from accredited and nonaccredited investors. The company, which produces vodka, gin, whiskey and fruit liqueurs, also borrowed from a regional bank.

It is this kind of success that has attracted entrepreneurs like Dillon Dakota Carroll to crowdfunding, even as the S.E.C. continues to drag its heels. Mr. Carroll's company, Levaté of Oklahoma City, has developed a lift device for wheelchairs. It is securing $200,000 from angel investors and is looking to raise $30,000 in a Kickstarter campaign.

For its next financing round, Mr. Carroll, 23, said he hoped to raise $1 million using Lendoor, a crowdfunding platform for small business loans, and financing through a combination of government grants and additional investments. A bank loan, however, is probably not an option.

"No traditional lending institution is going to want to give to any new start-up that doesn't have any sales yet," he said.

ZPM Espresso and the Rage of the Jilted Crowdfunder

BY GIDEON LEWIS-KRAUS | APRIL 30, 2015

"THANK YOU ALL VERY MUCH," Update 57 concluded, by way of goodbye. "Working on this project was the most ambitious and meaningful undertaking any of us have ever attempted. Getting to know all of you, and working to create some seriously cool technology, was one of the most rewarding things we've ever done. We are deeply and truly sorry that despite our best efforts, we were not able to get this machine across the finish line. Love, Gleb, Igor and Janet, Team ZPM."

It had been three long years of gradual disappointment since the 1,500 or so supporters of ZPM Espresso — otherwise known as the PID-Controlled Espresso Machine project on the crowdfunding platform Kickstarter — each put a few hundred dollars, or some $370,000 in total, into the campaign, and eight months since the last communiqué from the project's creators. Now, with Update 57 in January, ZPM Espresso announced that it was winding itself down. For the backers who expected a ZPM machine for their pledge, there would be neither fulfillment nor refunds. All accumulated moneys, the update said, were dispersed on the nonrecoverable engineering costs involved in ZPM's failed attempt to manufacture an inexpensive commercial-grade espresso machine for the home market.

Ian Woodhouse, the 44-year-old director of operations for a Toronto real estate developer, was one of ZPM's earliest and most ardent backers. Three years on, though, no new blow could surprise him. The update represented exactly what he had long come to expect from the creators. It was evasive and opaque. There was no clear explanation for the company's insolvency. Woodhouse was especially nettled by that valediction: "love." What he wanted, he told me later, was not another update "signed 'love.' They always signed their updates 'love.'" He could see that it seemed like a peculiar fixation, but the word was so disingenuous and cloying, and it made him angry. "Notice," he instructed me, "how I keep bringing up the 'love' thing." It reminded him that what ought to have been a straightforward financial transaction had somehow left him feeling taken advantage of and betrayed.

Powerless to act individually, the backers began, in Update 57's wake, to organize. Their first step was a Facebook group, "Ripped off by ZPM Espresso," but Woodhouse feared it wasn't private: The principals of ZPM, who seemed to him at once inept and robust in their malfeasance, might easily monitor the activity there. So Woodhouse, along with a few others among the more persistent backers, instead set up a private forum on the messaging service Slack, where they shared their sense of affliction and pondered legal or moral redress. The legal options were limited. Although Kickstarter's terms of use stipulate that any creators unable to satisfy the terms of their agreement with their backers might be subject to legal action, no sane attorney would initiate a class-action suit on a contingency-fee basis against insolvent creators, and no sane backer would ante up the necessary legal fees.

The other alternative was a consumer-protection suit filed by a state attorney general, but for that to proceed, the backers would need evidence of actual fraud, which they spent an enormous amount of time and energy trying to uncover. As Woodhouse, who speaks in the tone of a reasonable man drawn hopelessly against his will into a vast conspiracy, put it to me, "We found out a whole bunch of interesting information." He ticked off the names of four lawyers, an unpaid accountant and two Silicon Valley investors. He delved into what he dug up in the corporate-filings section of the State of Georgia's website, and on a shady-seeming portal seeking to bundle Chinese angel investments. By his estimations, ZPM had ultimately raised $1.2 million, all of it gone and unaccounted for. The ZPM founders, the backers discovered in their attempt to serve up (at the very least) a small-claims action, were lying low; they had left Atlanta and absconded for San Francisco.

Everything Woodhouse could find out, however, was "essentially hearsay," he said. He was exasperated. As someone involved in the project from its beginning, he felt entitled to know everything. Why did the creators never reveal that the project's founding engineer left the company for another job? Why were the other founders scrubbing their social-media profiles of connections to ZPM? Woodhouse had been caching screen shots, updates and videos to make sure the remaining data weren't similarly disappeared.

As the backers exchanged theories in private, matters were quick to escalate. Woodhouse registered the web addresses glebpolyakov.com and janettambasco.com — the names of the two lead ZPM founders. He did it, he explained, "because I wanted to have something of value to them." By then, it seemed to him that the only possible path to accountability was public shame. In response, on Kickstarter, Polyakov posted that he wished Woodhouse hadn't done something so needlessly personal. To Woodhouse, this was yet another sign that the creators had all the leverage. Woodhouse was anonymous on Kickstarter, and Polyakov could have linked him to the domain names, he surmised, only if the private group was compromised — indeed, infiltrated.

Since Kickstarter's debut in 2009, campaigns on the platform have raised $1.4 billion for the creators of more than 80,000 projects. In the process, the company and its crowdfunding competitors have invented a new sort of economic relationship, and a corresponding frontier of Internet acrimony. Disgruntled crowdfunders are not your typical Internet-commenting degenerates: In ZPM's case, they are affluent, well-educated professionals, working in New York and Los Angeles as systems analysts, TV directors, research physicians specializing in adrenal pathology — the sorts of people you would expect to write off their $250 donation as a gamble gone sour. Yet they found, for reasons that weren't always clear to them, that they couldn't. A professor in Columbia's graduate school of architecture wrote, on the private Slack forum, that he considered Polyakov to have "neither humility nor shame." He continued, "I also think it entirely appropriate that he never work in technology, finance, consulting or the coffee fields (sorry, that kills the barista career) again."

The rancor is due, perhaps, to a fundamental confusion about what crowdfunding really is. On one hand, a backer is not a customer, because the product does not exist yet and may never; Kickstarter is constantly reminding its patrons that the platform is not a store. (On some level, backers must already know this, or else they wouldn't be backers; if Ian Woodhouse had just wanted an inexpensive espresso machine, the top seller on Amazon retails for $86 and has thousands of five-star reviews.)

On the other hand, though, neither is a backer an investor, even if many of ZPM's backers insisted they be treated as such. A Kickstarter pledge does not buy a portion of a company. Backers do not sit on the board; they are not enfranchised to review the company's audited financials. Investors' interests, at least ideally, are aligned with those of the company, whereas nothing in the crowdfunding relationship ties a backer to the company for the long term. Moreover, the last thing Kickstarter wants to deal with is S.E.C. regulations.

In the platform's early days, Kickstarter's founders hardly imagined that a situation like this would arise. Neither was a technologist — Perry Chen, now 38, was an artist and gallerist, and Yancey Strickler, 36, was a music journalist — and although several of their recent hires have engineering backgrounds, they continue to see Kickstarter as something of an arts institution. Their office building, in Brooklyn's Greenpoint neighborhood, is a remodeled pencil factory where thousands of square feet are given over to a gallery, a theater and a shadowy, silent library. During the platform's initial phase, it did support some manufactured objects (simple iPhone cases, for example), but it wasn't until 2010, when the founders were faced with an iPhone tripod proposal, that they had to decide if such commercial projects qualified as "creative" in the way they intended. As Strickler remembers it, the tripod's creators responded that their particular tools happened to be injection molding and AutoCAD software, but that their enterprise was absolutely in the spirit of the platform. Kickstarter agreed to host the project, but that decision inspired a sustained effort to shape best practices for gadget campaigns. Its new rules included a requirement that there be a working prototype, and a prohibition on fancy computer renderings. (A spokesman for Kickstarter noted that if ZPM had listed its project today, it would have had to work hard to bring its pitch up to that standard.)

Until last October, Kickstarter's terms of use stipulated that project creators had only two options to discharge their obligations: ship or refund. Today, in response to situations like ZPM's, creators can refund, ship or explain, and if a full audit — financial or narrative — shows that the creators have made "every reasonable effort" toward a decent outcome, the backers are encouraged to feel satisfied. Strickler told me he feels it undermines the whole concept of crowdfunding to guarantee that products will be delivered or that refund money will be held in escrow; the acceptance of some risk, after all, is an integral part of patronage. "We wanted to protect a creator who makes an honest effort and comes up short," he told me. "We wanted to reserve legal efforts for real bad-actor behavior."

Even arts projects, of course, sometimes fall through. In December 2009, for example, the musician Josh Dibb (a member of Animal Collective) raised $26,000 to travel to Mali and record an album; six years on, his backers have yet to enjoy a single limited-edition-LP chord. A documentary filmmaker I spoke with raised more than $100,000 in 2012 to make a film about happiness in the Himalayas; he is drained from the effort of trying to explain himself to his backers. But the problem is especially acute with devices. The Wharton School professor Ethan Mollick, who has published several papers on crowdfunding, has found that more than 80 percent of hardware projects ship with significant delays. Most of those do ultimately deliver something, but Mollick has found that 14 percent of the projects studied have, since 2012, shipped either nothing at all or something too shoddy to use. An entire new consulting industry has in turn grown up to help crowdfund products. Just last month, Kickstarter unveiled a new section of its site, Campus, where creators can share hard-won advice and concerns.

The policy change has made things cleaner for Kickstarter when projects fail, but it arguably has complicated the creator-backer dynamic. If backers lack an absolute right to a product, and their legal options are limited, the policy only heightens their feeling of entitlement to full disclosure. "I long ago gave up on getting a machine, but I want my $250 of information," Woodhouse told me. Backers feel they are part of an Internet community that has been not merely disillusioned but somehow also rendered unreal, and they get worked up to know how they were let down. The sense of broad collective purpose that makes any given Kickstarter campaign compelling is exactly what can make it, for backers and creators alike, especially dangerous.

On March 16, Gleb Polyakov and Janet Tambasco, each 26, sat on either side of me in an empty San Francisco cafe. It was the sort of laminate-floored, Mayan-mural-walled joint that could still afford rent but couldn't afford one of the high-status, Ducati-looking contraptions with which ZPM sought to compete. The coffee wasn't great, but it was free-refill plentiful, and they'd been a little wary about giving out their current mailing address. Recently one backer, an engineer and father of four who spent time on the phone with them offering design advice and kept a very religious Christian household, doxxed Tambasco's mother, posting her personal information to a public Kickstarter thread. Polyakov and Tambasco had schlepped a Perspex box full of beta machines in various stages of dishabille.

"I wish the backers weren't so mean," Polyakov said.

Tambasco nodded. "I wish we'd done a better job."

The worst part, Tambasco continued, "is that the coffee machine works, and has always worked. It does what we said it would do. People are still emailing us to ask how to buy it." She assumed alternating whines. " 'I see your website is down. *How can I buy it?*' 'I saw your most recent update about how you failed. *How can I buy it?*' "

Polyakov is tall and stocky, with a wide, round face and hooded hazel eyes that suggest, in a cultured St. Petersburg family, the lingering threat of some ancestral steppe horseman. Tambasco is half-Italian and petite, with a dusky voice, profuse dark hair, vexed eyebrows and dark, shining eyes; like Polyakov, she makes an immediate impression of great intelligence, hers feisty and quilled even in her post-traumatic delirium. Without even once interrupting or talking over each other, they spent a few hours alternating their way through the story of how they ended up broke and vilified. Tambasco wore two layers of faded-fern military fatigue jackets and high, zippered black combat boots over scruffy leggings; Polyakov, a light beige sweater and thin dress slacks. Although it was 75 degrees and sunny, Tambasco cupped her gigantic, bitter black coffee with both hands for warmth. The scene was far removed from the remote and starlit tiki lounge in the backers' imaginations, where she sipped umbrellaed drinks.

Polyakov met ZPM's original engineer, Igor Zamlinsky, when they were children in Atlanta's Russian-Jewish émigré community. In Russia, their parents were artists and scientists; in Atlanta, Polyakov helped his mother run a "European" deli, which provisioned Atlanta's expat scene with everything Continental, from weisswurst to stuffed cabbage. He was born on Sakhalin, a Siberian island where his mother was doing climatology research. He grew up in St. Petersburg and came to the States when he was 5. In high school, he and Zamlinsky split their time between the garage, where they disassembled appliances and played with chemistry sets, and the local coffee shop, where the espresso they chain-drank gave the air an aroma of lost cosmopolitan sophistication. In 2011, Zamlinsky, during his senior year of college, resurrected a crude but effective espresso machine he once jury-rigged from spare parts, and that summer, the two sat around tetchy and overcaffeinated, lobbing possible business ideas back and forth. The least contrived and lame idea they came up with was to sell their coffee, or rather their machine itself.

Unlike any espresso machine then available for either the home or the commercial market, Zamlinsky's device used a cheap microcontroller ($20 off the shelf at RadioShack), along with an innovative pump design, to provide exacting digital control over pressure and temperature. Nearly everybody agrees that when it isn't on the fritz, the coffee it produces is excellent, perhaps even as good as shots pulled from the sculptural chrome La Marzoccos on every grounds-strewn marble countertop from La Colombe to Intelligentsia.

Polyakov thought Kickstarter was the likeliest place to scrounge up $20,000. That would allow them to buy a milling machine and set up a backyard foundry. If they were willing to discount to zero the value of their own labor, and put materials costs on their credit cards, they could hand-assemble 50 prototype units and price them at $200 apiece without losing all that much money. For help with their initial pitch, they drafted Tambasco, a high-school friend with a degree from Princeton in molecular biology and a minor in creative writing; she studied under Joyce Carol Oates. The trio shot a bumbling sales-pitch video of great charm, which ought to have dispelled any doubts that the two principals were anything but echt engineers. On Dec. 10, 2011, Polyakov pressed publish on their campaign and went to bed.

When they woke up, they discovered that they had already raised $10,000. Their campaign then got picked up by a well-respected coffee blog, and they achieved the $20,000 goal within the first day. They closed out their second day at $32,000. The tech blog Gizmodo wrote that they "might not suck," and Kickstarter featured them on its front page.

With Zamlinsky in the garage tinkering with machine design, and Polyakov frantic on the phone with contractors and suppliers in seven countries, they needed somebody to deal with the front end. During the initial Kickstarter campaign alone, they received more than 4,000 emails (more than a few of them, even then, in all caps). Tambasco had never intended to make ZPM customer service a full-time job, much less a three-year source of dark and deepening hollows under her eyes, but somebody had to answer those emails and write the updates. In late January, their campaign closed with $370,000 in pledges, of which they went on to collect about $330,000. They were the sixth-most-funded Kickstarter project to date. They had 1,500 orders to fill.

A chief tenet of the Internet age is belief in the natural proliferation of democracy and decentralization, in the ability of distributed networks of everyday people to achieve what once required top-down hierarchies and a great concentration of power. When you contribute to a Kickstarter campaign that funds an album or a documentary, you're participating in the creation of cultural value outside the risk-averse bureaucracies of mass cultural production. You're kicking in to cut out the middlemen of music labels or Hollywood studios.

The same goes for gadgets, perhaps even more so: You could always record an album in your basement, after all, but it's only recently that a novice outfit might attempt industrial-scale appliance production. Projects like the Oculus Rift virtual-reality headset or the Pebble watch (both of which were Kickstarter successes that went on to become big independent businesses; the former was acquired last year by Facebook for $2 billion) course with a special energy that derives from the exchange of far-flung resources among the sympathetic and like-minded. The realized object takes on a kind of totemic significance through the aspirations and the values of the community that brought it into being. It's not some black box made elsewhere and delivered overnight. The backer feels less like a passive consumer than a proud co-conspirator.

At the same time, like all 21st-century consumers, Kickstarter backers have been trained to expect a world custom-engineered for total frictionlessness. Everything is supposed to work easily, right away and well. One benefit of giving our lives over to machines and algorithms, after all, is that there's no margin for human error. As for our physical objects, we expect them to be sleek and perfect, designed with a religious devotion to the harmony of form and function. It's no accident that the most common way people refer to the industrial-design studio at Apple, with its prototypes hidden from visitors under white shrouds, is as a temple. This is a kind of perfection created under the auspices of the old model: high priests, secret tabernacles, inherited authorities, management by diktat.

My brother has worked at Apple for 10 years, first in operations and now in engineering. I asked him what advice he would have given to Polyakov if he'd been called in to consult on the manufacturing. He thought for a minute. "I honestly haven't the faintest idea," he said. This is because, despite all the advances of the maker-revolution age (off-the-shelf, open-source, programmable microcontrollers; rapid prototyping; 3-D printing; "AutoCAD for Dummies"), manufacturing remains a supremely difficult process, the success of which continues to rely on marshaling a lot of resources: development money, an extensive network of trusted vendors, the dedicated personnel to sit in conference rooms in concrete campuses in Shenzhen and Dongguan and refuse to budge until the product is streaming off the assembly line in the right amounts, at the right quality and at the agreed-upon price.

On the fourth day of their campaign, the ZPM team pushed the machine's estimated delivery date back three months, from March 2012 to June. Even if they were willing to spend years crouched in painstaking garage assembly, there was just no way to get the parts they needed off the shelf. It is fiendishly difficult to produce 2,000 of anything, which is the number of machines ZPM ultimately had to come up with. Two thousand units neither brings you to the point where you're realizing the major benefits of economies of scale nor gives you sufficient volume to have any leverage in negotiations over price, schedule and quality. As Polyakov put it, "You sort of have to make 2,000 of something to find out if you can make 2,000 of something."

With small runs, the cost per unit can balloon. ZPM's second manufacturer, San Diego's D&K, told the founders their engineering drawings weren't adequate and presented them with overage fees totaling $100,000. Pending payment, Polyakov says, D&K is still holding the consigned parts and assembled machines hostage. (D&K declined to comment on the matter.)

If ZPM's backers eventually felt jilted, it was not because the "love" of ZPM's leave-taking was fake but because that love had once been fully requited. In an initial survey conducted at the immediate close of the campaign, 34 percent of backers identified as engineers or computer scientists, and many of them expected to be able to offer their own expertise along the way, and perhaps to learn a little about manufacturing on the side. ZPM's 56 regular updates included pictures and videos, all of them punning and intimate. One of the project's backers commented on three different updates that it was a real treat to receive the founders' "National Geographic tales of the travels to China, and such," and said he looked forward to relating those anecdotes for years over espressos from his machine. Even as the company's struggles began, some backers did provide genuine help. "There was Doug, at the sheet-metal facility," Tambasco recalled, "and Colin, who helped us with the pressure sensors." There was a design professor who flew in for the day to help with the user interface.

Eventually, though, the advice became overwhelming. "They're doing it on their own schedule, nights and weekends, taking up a huge amount of Igor's time when he's got a ton of work to do," she said. "People got insulted because they couldn't be involved as much as they wanted." The ongoing calls for transparency put pressure on ZPM to carry on all of its business in public, but transparency and efficacy can be incommensurable ideals. ZPM couldn't blame its vendors in updates, even for the mistakes they were consistently making, if the company wanted to keep working with them — or with anyone at all. The backers had a hard time understanding this; they continued to operate under the shared assumption that more democracy, more engagement and more transparency lead inexorably to more success.

Furthermore, ZPM had nothing to say when its vendors adjusted their own timelines based on backer support. Each time ZPM announced another delay, most of the backers would respond in a friendly tone. (No worries, thanks for keeping us up to date!) The vendors would point to those comments to argue there was no great rush. ZPM also could not publish a full financial audit, because open books make meaningful cost negotiation impossible. "I just can't publish our financials, our cost breakdown," Tambasco said. "If I do that then when I go to get this thing made, then everybody knows how much I have in the bank. Then what they're going to do is just drain that money."

Which is exactly what happened. With the momentum from the project's successful Kickstarter, ZPM sold another $230,000 worth of machines as online preorders; the founders hoped the extra cash would make for a better final product. Then, when they ran low on funds again, they raised another $285,000 from angel investors — which, though the founders saw the action as part of a good-faith effort to deliver on their promises, effectively broke their original covenant with the crowdfunding community. They also hired outside consultants on retainer — paid professionals who were, in spirit, the very opposite of backers, since they had no extramonetary commitment to ZPM's success. When one of those consultants demanded, in the spring of 2014, that the project act like a "real start-up" and go into what people in Silicon Valley often call "stealth mode," the updates came to an abrupt halt. The founders hoped that by posting their email addresses and phone numbers, and offering to field queries and complaints in person, they might assuage the backer community, but this plan, in hindsight, seemed misbegotten. It only confirmed for the backers that their one plank of accountability — the public nature of the story on offer — had been withdrawn.

ZPM's silence drove the backers into a tizzy. Despite the deranged conspiracy-mongering ideas to which some of them ultimately clung, the reality of ZPM's failure was pretty banal: The founders were naïve and inexperienced, well intentioned but clumsy, and they serially trusted and paid the wrong people for ineffective help. Even when this was explained to the backers, they couldn't bring themselves to believe it. There were calls for Polyakov to go back to Russia, for him to rot in a Mexican prison. One backer continued to leave angry comments for more than a year after he received a refund. Other backers were gratified to find a Facebook picture that seemed to them incontrovertible proof that Polyakov and Tambasco were, or had been, carrying on a romantic relationship. It was as if the secrets withheld were taking place behind the keyhole of a parental bedroom. One backer "discovered" that Polyakov's father must be Alexander Polyakov, a physicist at Princeton, and that this connection had to have something or other to do with his and Tambasco's hidden relationship. (Alexander Polyakov has no relation to Gleb Polyakov; Gleb's father, Mark Polyakov, was a computer programmer in the Soviet Union. Gleb and his mother left Russia in 1994, when Mark was murdered in a mugging on their doorstep.)

The virtual family having broken up, there was a scramble to claim the household items. Woodhouse himself, who frequently described his crusade as one of solidarity with those who shelled out money they couldn't spare on a luxury item that was only ever theoretical in the first place, emailed Polyakov right after Update 57, to say: "Do you still have the development or beta machines? If so, is there any way we could work something out to get one to me?" He concluded mildly, "I'm sorry the project came to this, but I understand the complexities." (Woodhouse claims he was just trying to get Polyakov's attention.)

When a crowdfunded project comes together — as, after all, a vast majority of these campaigns do — a great sense of collective achievement swells. People talk about their first-generation Pebble watches the way they talk about a hometown sweetheart who made it big in pictures. Pebble watches and Oculus Rifts are, of course, the outliers, but even the minor wins remind us that there are times when we all prove capable of rising to an Internet occasion. There's a form of enchantment that results when a diverse community, materializing from nothing, gets behind an act of creation that no other institution would support.

But in ZPM's case, the enchantment was long ago irretrievably dispelled. Once the money was finally gone, and the project's consultant had bolted with engineers in tow, the founders' only option was to hope somebody might buy what remained of the company and deliver them from their moral (and, possibly, legal) commitments. They knew it would be a tough sell: They had a technology at last viable for mass production, but they were also lugging around hundreds of thousands of dollars in liabilities. Their backers, sending comments and emails into the void, had always felt a lack of leverage, but now Polyakov and Tambasco were in something of the same position. They walked into rooms with their backs already against the wall.

In early March 2015, Tambasco posted a brief new update, No. 58, to the effect that the founders were in negotiations to sell ZPM. Their suitor was John Buckman, a 45-year-old serial entrepreneur and the outgoing chairman of the Electronic Frontier Foundation; he had himself been expecting a ZPM machine for some years now and was a member of Woodhouse's private group.

I joined Polyakov on a trip to Buckman's home in San Rafael, about half an hour north of the Golden Gate Bridge. Buckman lives on a narrow private road up a large hill, with floor-to-ceiling windows and nobody to see from them. He greeted us as though he'd just been tugged gently back to earth from a low-grade levitation session. The walls of his aerie were cream-colored and without adornment, except for five Renaissance lutes hanging in formation on a faux-Egyptian tapestry.

Buckman was drawn to ZPM because he "hadn't yet seen someone marrying computers and espresso powerfully." He uses a state-of-the-art VacMaster VP215 Chamber Vacuum Sealer to cache his meals; his fridge, packed with rows of baggied tuber, legume and flesh, resembles an evidence locker in an organ-theft investigation. In the garage, beside his matching Segways, he has a freezer that goes to minus 6 degrees — regular freezers don't keep his fish sufficiently gelid — and a steel sous-vide basin that heats his VacMastered bags to temperatures accurate to one-tenth of a degree. His pantry countertop has a line of 13 power outlets. Polyakov set up his machine, and, once he got the calibration right, we sampled a series of amphetaminic shots.

At the end of our day, Buckman sat loosely lotus-legged under the algaelike jasmine on his deck, the setting sun at his back. The light was in Polyakov's face, and he had to squint into the jasmine. There was not a whole lot to discuss. The backers suspected that Polyakov would try to sell the intellectual property and pocket the proceeds, but in fact Polyakov's total asking price for the company was $35,000 to settle the founders' legal and professional debts, equity consideration for their angel investors and, most important, a guarantee that Buckman would honor ZPM's commitment to its backers.

Buckman, understandably, did not want to accept liabilities that might put his home at risk, but he had spent a lot of time on the phone with such "trolls" as Woodhouse, he said, and thought he had found a way forward: He would issue each backer a coupon for a credit toward the final machine, at the value of the backer's initial pledge. He would make a thin margin on the first 2,000 machines the company owed, but he would also have an attractive redemption story, and 2,000 evangelists for his new venture. Woodhouse, who was enlisted as an adviser, was fine with the whole idea. Buckman and Polyakov agreed broadly on terms, and ZPM would soon turn over all of the engineering files needed to reproduce the machine.

In April, though, even this shot at deliverance seemed to drain away. Buckman was airing many of the same grievances that the backers had: Polyakov was disorganized and confusing and opaque in his communications. Unlike the backers, Buckman had the resources to move forward on his own, and unlike Polyakov, he had no one to hold him to account. He was going to start his own company to build a home espresso machine. His new company, he told Polyakov at one point, would be called Decent Coffee.

GIDEON LEWIS-KRAUS is a contributing writer for the magazine and the author of "A Sense of Direction: Pilgrimage for the Restless and the Hopeful." He last wrote about the director Christopher Nolan.

S.E.C. Gives Small Investors Access to Equity Crowdfunding

BY STACY COWLEY | OCT. 30, 2015

ENTREPRENEURS RAISING MONEY through crowdfunding campaigns have typically rewarded their backers with early access to products and with tchotchkes like T-shirts and coffee mugs.

But under new rules adopted Friday by the Securities and Exchange Commission, they will be able to offer a prize that could be more lucrative: an equity stake in their business.

The rules will allow small investors to buy shares of private companies under the provisions of the Jump-Start Our Business Start-Ups Act. Until the change, equity crowdfunding had been legal only for accredited investors, or those who met required levels of assets and income.

President Obama called the bill, better known as the JOBS Act, "a potential game-changer" for fledgling companies, when he signed it more than three years ago. But the law stalled as regulators struggled to write rules stringent enough to protect investors but flexible enough to allow for meaningful fund-raising.

A set of draft rules released two years ago was widely criticized and deemed almost unworkable by many in the industry, who said that compliance would be too costly and complex. The rules adopted Friday had been substantially revised to address some of those concerns.

The new rules allow companies to raise up to $1 million in a 12-month period through a crowdfunding campaign. Companies will need to provide their potential investors with financial statements, but some first-time issuers and those seeking less than $500,000 will not be required to have the statements audited — an important concession for those concerned about the cost of providing audited financials.

Companies will be able to advertise their offerings in a variety of ways, including posting them on Kickstarter-like portals for investors to peruse. (Kickstarter has said that it is not interested in expanding into equity crowdfunding, though one of its top rivals, Indiegogo, said it is considering doing so.)

Dozens of investment portals have sprung up in recent years, but until now, only accredited investors — those with an annual income exceeding $200,000 or a net worth of at least $1 million — have been permitted to invest in most of the deals advertised on them.

Some of those portals now plan to expand into the nonaccredited market. SeedInvest, a site that has helped 50 funding deals in the last three years, expects to begin offering deals next year to a wider pool of investors.

"There's no question that there's a lot of pent-up demand from ordinary investors," said Ryan Feit, the site's chief executive and one of its founders. "At the end of the day, that means there will be more capital available for small business."

The amount of money backers will be allowed to invest depends on their income. Those with an annual income or net worth of less than $100,000 will be allowed to invest up to $2,000 in a 12-month period, or 5 percent of the lesser of their income or net worth, whichever is greater. Those with an income and net worth of more than $100,000 will be permitted to invest up to 10 percent of the lesser of their annual income or net worth.

The equity shares they buy will be risky, illiquid investments. Investors will generally be required to hold on to the shares for at least one year, and there are not yet many marketplaces for those seeking to sell shares in private companies, which are difficult to value.

Some critics are deeply skeptical about the quality of the investments that will be available. "Ninety-nine percent of these deals will prove to be unprofitable," said Andrew Stoltmann, a lawyer who specializes in securities fraud. "This is a disaster waiting to happen."

Others counter that the new rules will allow entrepreneurs' family, friends, customers and professional contacts to invest in ventures that they want to support.

"I think it's going to really make a difference for businesses that are not especially fashionable for professional investors," said James Dowd, the chief executive of North Capital Private Securities, a broker-dealer that focuses on private fund-raising. "They want to invest in companies that have the potential to be disruptive to an entire industry. You don't see a lot of capital flow into ordinary consumer and retail businesses."

The S.E.C. on Friday also proposed changes to several other fund-raising rules, including those governing intrastate offerings. More than 25 states have adopted their own crowdfunding rules to let local businesses raise money from residents within the state, often with fewer regulatory requirements than the federal rules. The commission suggested striking down a rule that blocked those intrastate offerings from being advertised to out-of-state investors — a quirk that prevented companies from publicizing their fund-raising campaigns on their own websites or on social media sites.

"It's an absurd thing, but that's what the law said. It was horrifying," said Kendall Almerico, a lawyer who specializes in crowdfunding issues. "Fixing this is huge."

The range of ways in which private companies can raise money from nonaccredited investors has significantly expanded this year. In June, new federal rules took effect allowing companies to raise up to $50 million through a provision known as Regulation A. Those deals carry stricter disclosure and compliance requirements than the crowdfunding process outlined on Friday, which is intended to be much cheaper and faster for issuers.

Taken together, the new federal and state rules give entrepreneurs a much wider set of options for raising money from a diverse pool of investors.

"I'm surprised at how far the S.E.C. went to make it all work," said Douglas S. Ellenoff, a securities lawyer at Ellenoff Grossman & Schole. "The entrepreneur now has a series of very interesting choices and lots of different options for how they go about their capital formation."

The S.E.C.'s four commissioners voted 3-1 on Friday morning to adopt the new crowdfunding rules, which are expected to take effect early next year.

Global Brands, Taking Cue From Tinkerers, Explore Crowdfunding

BY STACY COWLEY | JAN. 6, 2016

THE OPAL NUGGET ICE MAKER machine had all the usual hallmarks of a crowdfunded hit, aside from one tiny bit of fine print.

The countertop device for making chewable ice shards was one of the most heavily funded projects last year on Indiegogo, raising nearly $2.8 million from more than 6,000 contributors. Engineers from FirstBuild, the project's creator, posted videos of their design prototype, filmed inside a tool-strewn workshop, and talked openly about the remaining technical challenges before their machine would be ready for delivery in mid-2016.

It looked like a typical invention dreamed up by a scrappy team seeking cash for manufacturing — except that FirstBuild is a subsidiary of General Electric.

Crowdfunding, a trend popularized by artists and tinkerers, is now so hot that corporate giants are looking for a way in. G.E.'s approach is an unusually bold one, but a growing number of large companies are experimenting with programs intended to capture some of the creativity and passion that popular crowdfunded projects can inspire.

Indiegogo, one of the largest fund-raising sites, on Wednesday announced "enterprise crowdfunding," a new offering for big brands. For a consulting fee that typically runs to six figures, Indiegogo will help companies figure out how to harness the crowd's power.

"The conversations are very similar to the ones companies were having 15 years ago about social media — like, déjà vu," said Jerry Needel, Indiegogo's head of revenue and corporate partnerships. "It's not just, 'We want to run a campaign, give us some best practices and we'll go do the rest.' It's much more early stage. It's, 'What should we do? What can we do? Let's figure it out.' "

In many cases, major brands are investing their resources in the work of independent entrepreneurs.

Philip Petracca and his business partners, a group of self-described "beer geeks," raised $234,000 on Indiegogo last year to create the Fizzics Beer System, a device that uses a sound-wave generator to give canned or bottled beer a foam like draft beer. As they prepared to ship the first batch, they went looking for a retailer to bring it to a mass audience.

A meeting with Brookstone quickly led to a deal. The $170 Fizzics machine was one of the retailing chain's best-selling holiday items and helped pioneer a process that the company recently formalized with its Brookstone Launch development program for fledgling products.

Some participants, like Fizzics, simply want Brookstone to sell their goods. Others are looking for a more extensive partnership.

When Wenqing Yan, a recent college graduate, sketched out her concept for cat-ear headphones with glowing lights, she had a hunch the idea would be popular. But when 20,000 backers pledged $3.4 million to the project, Ms. Yan and her business partner, Victoria Hu, found themselves facing a much greater manufacturing challenge than they had anticipated.

"I'm not an engineer, and neither is my co-founder," said Ms. Hu, who obtained a degree in political economy from the University of California, Berkeley. "We were searching pretty actively for more professional help."

Brookstone spotted the project and reached out. Ms. Hu initially ignored the message, but after a production deal in China fell apart, she agreed to talk. With her and Ms. Yan's blessing, the company took over nearly all aspects of the project, including the manufacturing, shipping and customer service.

Brookstone, which filed for bankruptcy in 2014 and restructured under new ownership, hopes the creations that emerge from Brookstone Launch will be a cornerstone of its product portfolio.

"One of our priorities is to expand our innovation pipeline," said Thomas M. Via, Brookstone's chief executive. "Crowdfunding seemed to be a natural place for us to go. We're counting on these unique items to be a growing percentage of our overall revenue."

The crowdfunding ventures of big brands tend to fall into two distinct categories. A very few, like G.E., have sought money directly. The Kickstarter campaign of the "Veronica Mars" movie raised eyebrows when fans realized that their money would be going straight into the coffers of Warner Bros. — but they still contributed $5.7 million.

A more popular option is to solicit ideas from the masses. The grocery retailer FreshDirect ran a contest on RocketHub for new food products, and Hasbro used Indiegogo to seek party game concepts. The Shock Top beer brand from Anheuser-Busch InBev sponsored a campaign for new inventions to combat California's drought.

Both approaches can be risky. Just as with social media, where brands routinely humiliate themselves, the potential for coming off as tone-deaf is high — and backers may not be inclined to participate when they know that a project's creator has deep pockets. A Honda campaign on Indiegogo to preserve drive-in movie theaters collected only around half of the $100,000 it sought.

Kickstarter, the biggest project crowdfunding site, is ambivalent about the rise in corporate enthusiasm. While Kickstarter does not bar big brands from using its site, it has not made any effort to cater to them. The projects it has hosted for well-known creators tend to be public-minded, like the Smithsonian's effort to preserve Neil Armstrong's spacesuit.

"Creators of all shapes and sizes are welcome on Kickstarter," said David Gallagher, a Kickstarter spokesman. "Backers ultimately decide what does well on Kickstarter, and they typically look for creators who are trying something genuinely new and creative."

Ethan Mollick, a crowdfunding researcher at the Wharton School of the University of Pennsylvania, thinks that is a very tricky pitch for big brands to pull off.

"These are not normal transactions," Mr. Mollick said. "Everyone concentrates too much on 'funding' and not enough on 'crowd.' These are people investing in you because they want to believe in you, and to believe that you need their help."

G.E. acknowledges a few misfires in its FirstBuild crowdfunding experiments — but not the ones it anticipated.

The company, which spends $5 billion a year on research and development, got very little negative reaction for shaking the donation jar on Indiegogo to fund its product preorders, according to Natarajan Venkatakrishnan, FirstBuild's director. The Opal ice maker, FirstBuild's second crowdfunded product, significantly exceeded its $150,000 funding target.

But the backers did not just want a device to eventually arrive in their mailboxes. They wanted to feel involved in and informed about its development.

"They want a personal email in their inbox every couple of weeks," Mr. Venkatakrishnan said. "That's something we're still trying to find a balance on."

As brands pile in and attach themselves to crowdfunding successes, the original backers of successful projects sometimes feel squeezed out. It is like finding that your favorite indie band has gone corporate and booked a stadium tour.

"Look at what happened with Oculus Rift," Mr. Mollick said, referring to the virtual reality start-up that raised $2.4 million on Kickstarter, and was then acquired by Facebook for $2 billion. "There was a real sense of betrayal."

For some entrepreneurs, though, going mass-market is not a risk — it is the entire goal.

Fizzics, based in Newark, gave Brookstone a few months of sales exclusivity in the United States, but in March, it plans to begin selling its machine through several more national retailers. The company also sees a commercial fit for its device at any place that serves beer, like breweries and sports bars.

"This is a whole new category that we're building," Mr. Petracca said. "We're working on products with lower price points, and we're working on a higher-end product that does some very unique things."

He isn't worried about big brands overrunning the crowdfunding market. One day, he intends for his company to be one of them.

New Crowdfunding Rules Let the Small Fry Swim With Sharks

BY STACY COWLEY | MAY 14, 2016

IF YOU'VE ALWAYS DREAMED of being Mr. Wonderful from "Shark Tank," now is your chance.

Starting Monday, new rules will permit anyone, not just the moneyed, to risk $2,000 a year or more investing in small companies in exchange for a stake in the business. Companies can raise up to $1 million a year this way.

This change, years in the making, represents an enormous shift, one that essentially permits anyone to become a venture capitalist — with all the attendant risks of losing one's shirt on a company that fails. Until now, only accredited investors, meaning those with an annual income of at least $200,000 or a net worth of at least $1 million,

BRYAN ANSELM FOR THE NEW YORK TIMES

Kelechi Anyadiegwu, 26, founded Zuvaa, an online African fashion marketplace. She plans to raise money through crowdfunding.

have been permitted to take equity stakes in most private companies. The wealthy "sharks" of the ABC reality television series got to risk their money, while the rest of us watched the action from the couch.

It is also an opportunity for start-ups and other small businesses, which can raise money with fairly few regulatory burdens. For instance, small companies seeking less than $500,000 and most first-time issuers will not need to provide audited financial statements, just unaudited ones.

"For the first time, ordinary Americans will be able to go online and invest in entrepreneurs that they believe in," President Obama said when he signed the bill into law that set these changes in motion.

That was four years ago. It took a long time to iron out the details, in part because the Securities and Exchange Commission was concerned that ordinary people could lose their life savings because of fraud or naïveté.

That remains a fear for many in the financing industry. Samuel Asher Effron, a lawyer with Mintz, Levin, Cohn, Ferris, Glovsky and Popeo who specializes in securities law, thinks the companies that choose to crowdfund will largely be those that are passed over by professional investors.

"When high-growth companies are looking to raise money, it's not just for the money," he said. "They're also looking for validation, and they want it from venture funds or well-known angels. They won't get that from a crowdfunding offer."

But one entrepreneur who is eager to take advantage of the new rules is Kelechi Anyadiegwu, 26, who started Zuvaa, an online marketplace of African fashions, two years ago. Her website is a portal where African-inspired designers from around the world can market their wares, which recently included a $120 office-appropriate dress from Tanzania and a $55 Lycra dashiki party dress.

When sales recently topped $1 million, she said, she started thinking about expanding. So far she has been relying on pop-up retail events, networking, and Instagram and Facebook accounts that now have more than 100,000 followers.

"We're building a tribe of women around the world who are passionate about African textiles and want to support these emerging designers," Ms. Anyadiegwu said.

It occurred to her that those women might be interested in buying not just dresses and textiles but also a piece of the company. Ms. Anyadiegwu has been talking to SeedInvest, one of about a dozen companies poised to serve as middlemen in the emerging business.

Ms. Anyadiegwu wants to increase her part-time workers' hours, move her base of operations from Sayreville, N.J., to Atlanta, where she has built a clientele, and do more marketing. To finance that, she's willing to part with some of her equity in the business.

"Our customer base is so engaged," she said. "This could be a perfect opportunity for them to participate and be a part of the company in another way."

Another company thinking about taking this route is Rorus, a technology start-up in Pittsburgh that makes water filters for developing countries. It has already raised nearly $300,000 from rich individuals and traditional venture capital funds, but the founders like the idea of building a larger circle of investors who act as advocates.

"We can build a community around our company. That's an intangible that you don't get from private fund-raising," said Kyle Henson, 23, the company's chief business officer. He is preparing Rorus to comply with the new securities rules, he said, if it chooses to do a crowdfunding offering.

But are the 230 million adult Americans who aren't millionaires really that interested in becoming do-it-yourself venture capitalists? While supporters cheer the new rules as a democratization of high finance, potentially opening up to the masses deals once reserved for the rich, skeptics worry that regular investors might get only the leftovers.

They may dream of discovering the next Facebook. But the most promising companies — the high-growth ventures delivering the monster returns that keep the entire venture-capital industry afloat — may also be the ones least likely to bother raising money in small dribs from the crowd, they fear.

FINDING 'BLOCKBUSTERS'

The shift toward the new rules began more than four years ago, when President Obama signed the Jump-Start Our Business Start-Ups Act, a bipartisan bill that he called a "potential game changer" for fledgling businesses. The bill itself is a slender 22-page document ordering a number of technical changes to ease fund-raising for small companies.

But what got people excited was the crowdfunding provision allowing companies to raise up to $1 million with few regulatory obstacles.

Sounds simple, right? Not to the Securities and Exchange Commission. Concerned about protecting investors from charlatans, bad ideas and their own poor judgment, the agency spent years drafting its proposed rules. The final version, released in October, runs to 685 pages.

The new rule, known as Regulation Crowdfunding, allows most private companies to advertise shares for sale to anyone, regardless of income. Individual investors can invest $2,000 to $100,000 a year in crowdfunding offerings, depending on their earnings and net worth.

The option appeals to Bhree Roumagoux, 42, and Robert Hensch, 46, a married couple in Anchorage who make a hobby of tracking early-stage technology ventures. They recently sank a five-figure sum into buying shares in Virtuix, a privately held start-up in Austin, Tex., that is developing a virtual reality motion platform for gaming.

The company caught Mr. Hensch's eye nearly two years ago, after it raised $1.1 million on Kickstarter. He scoured tech blogs for tidbits, signed up for the company's newsletter and followed along as executives posted updates from China about their production process.

So when Virtuix announced in March that it would crowdfund its next investment round, Mr. Hensch and Ms. Roumagoux jumped in. "I've seen where Robert's recommendations have gone in the market. Typically, when he identifies something early on, it becomes a blockbuster item," said Ms. Roumagoux, recalling her husband's early enthusiasm for Tesla, Netflix and a "really neat" search engine called Google.

Ms. Roumagoux works as a lawyer, and Mr. Hensch is a real estate business manager. As financiers, "we're definitely novices," she said with a laugh, but both like the idea of diversifying their retirement fund and other investments by gambling on a small portfolio of fledgling technology ventures.

Jan Goetgeluk, Virtuix's founder and chief executive, likes the idea of having hundreds or thousands of stakeholders along for the ride. "This allows us to turn those fans into true brand advocates. It's incredibly powerful."

Mr. Goetgeluk, a 32-year-old mechanical engineer, had dreamed of becoming an entrepreneur since moving to the United States from Belgium nine years ago. The money he raised from 3,000 backers on Kickstarter funded Virtuix's early production, and the publicity the

COLEY BROWN FOR THE NEW YORK TIMES

Some items offered by Zuvaa. Proceeds from Zuvaa's crowdfunding offering would be used for a corporate move and marketing, among other things.

campaign created got him a spot pitching his company to a panel of rich investors on "Shark Tank" — where he failed to land a deal.

"If my husband brought this into my house, I would divorce him immediately," Barbara Corcoran, a real estate entrepreneur, announced on the show.

Still, Mr. Goetgeluk went on to raise $8 million in two seed rounds from venture capitalists and wealthy angel investors, and an additional $4.7 million from a more complicated — and much more expensive — previous program for selling stock to regular investors.

The rules that take effect on Monday make crowdfunding far cheaper and easier for companies to use. But the cost of that concession is a $1 million cap on the amount they can raise in a 12-month period.

CAUTIONARY TALES

To promote their offerings, companies will have to work through a funding portal, a kind of online bazaar for investment deals. More than a dozen websites are preparing to enter the business, including CrowdBoarders, FlashFunders, NextSeed, SeedInvest, StartEngine and ZacksInvest.

Wefunder, one of the first to get a green light from regulators, says it will have around 20 live offerings on Monday. It's a day the site's creators, Mike Norman, Greg Belote and Nick Tommarello, thought might never come. They started their company in 2012, and then they waited.

"We had no idea that it would take the S.E.C. four years to write all these rules," Mr. Tommarello said. "We had to figure out how to stay alive and not go bankrupt."

To make money, the site started hosting Regulation D offerings — the kind only wealthy people can invest in. Some of those deals turned into cautionary tales. In 2013, the human resources start-up Zenefits raised money from Wefunder investors, who bought in at a valuation of $9 million. Two years later, the company's valuation had sailed past $4 billion.

And then, three months ago, Zenefits imploded. The company's founder and chief executive, Parker Conrad, stepped down after it was discovered that he had created software that let Zenefits employees cheat on a brokerage licensing course. Zenefits is being investigated by regulators in several states, faces fines that could total millions of dollars and risks even stiffer penalties. A valuation is hard to calculate on that kind of mess, but it's safe to say that the $4 billion days have passed.

Many start-ups that take crowdfunding money — probably most — will fail. Half of American small businesses close within their first five years, and even successful companies usually struggle through many lean years before generating meaningful profits.

That's one reason the S.E.C. moved so slowly. "We are counting on brokers and funding portals to be bulwarks of investor protection in this space," Mary Jo White, chairwoman of the S.E.C., said in a recent speech. "We will hold them to that responsibility."

Still, this isn't like investing in the stock market. Want to sell Facebook? Just call your broker. Want to sell your shares in Ms. Anyadiegwu's company, Zuvaa? Well, under the new crowdfunding rules, people must generally hold their shares for at least a year. And even then, there are few marketplaces for finding another buyer.

Virtuix's offering circular, which is a more detailed document than is required from companies using the new rules taking effect this week, is full of warnings. The company has not finished its commercial product, has little revenue and has a history of losses. It also has a "going concern" notice — the warning auditors put in when they're not sure that a company has enough cash to survive.

But Ms. Roumagoux, who said she had skimmed the circular, isn't worried. She and her husband may not be millionaires, but she says they're financially sophisticated enough to judge the risk that they're taking.

"I know all these rules are there to protect us, but honestly, I don't think we need the protection," she said. "We're relatively young, and this is a long-term investment."

Ever Wanted to Back a Start-Up? Indiegogo Opens the Door to Small Investors

BY STACY COWLEY | NOV. 15, 2016

ARMCHAIR VENTURE CAPITALISTS will soon have a new place to hunt for intriguing start-ups: Indiegogo, the popular crowdfunding site for developers of creative ventures like movies, games and gadgets.

Starting on Tuesday, the site will give entrepreneurs the option of offering backers an equity stake in their projects and creations. Indiegogo is the first major crowdfunding site to use a new securities rule that took effect six months ago, allowing ordinary investors to risk up to a few thousands dollars a year backing private companies.

Previously, only accredited investors — wealthy people with an annual income of more than $200,000 or a net worth of at least $1 million — were allowed to put money into such risky ventures. That created a schism: Companies like Pebble, a smartwatch maker, and Oculus, a virtual reality headset developer, raised millions on crowdfunding sites from eager early customers and used that surge to prove that buyers wanted their fledgling products.

But when those companies subsequently raised money from investors, crowdfunding backers were shut out. When Facebook acquired Oculus for $2 billion, venture capitalists and rich angel investors reaped the rewards.

"In a lot of ways, this levels the playing field," said David Mandelbrot, Indiegogo's chief executive. "This was one of the few areas of the law where citizens were treated differently based on the amount of wealth that they have."

Securities law had long prohibited regular investors from gambling on private companies because they can be risky investments that are likely to go bad. Half of American small businesses with employees shut down within five years, and those that survive often take many years to turn a profit. Things have not been looking so hot for Pebble, for example, which recently laid off a quarter of its staff.

Still, some entrepreneurs are eager to test out the new market. ArtCraft Entertainment, a video game developer in Austin, is considering an Indiegogo campaign to find investors for Crowfall, a game it plans to release next year.

Crowfall already took in nearly $1.8 million from a Kickstarter campaign last year. For that, the company offered traditional crowdfunding perks like early access to the game's beta tests and a thank you in Crowfall's credits.

Some 33,000 backers have kicked in money for Crowfall's development, and ArtCraft — which has also raised money from traditional early-stage investors — likes the idea of offering them a stake in the game's financial outcome, said J. Todd Coleman, the company's creative director.

The company considered an offering in May, when equity crowdfunding became legal, but backed off because of concerns about whether it could draw interest, Mr. Coleman said. Selling stakes to small investors is a strictly regulated process, and all offerings must be run through portals registered with the Financial Industry Regulatory Authority. Indiegogo is partnering with MicroVentures, a registered portal that will handle the back-end investment logistics.

Around 20 portals have become certified and started courting investors, but interest has been scant. Only 55 companies have run successful equity crowdfunding campaigns, raising a total of $12.4 million, according to statistics compiled by the investment portal Wefunder.

Indiegogo could shake up the field by bringing investment opportunities to a much wider audience. Some eight million people have backed projects on the site, raising more than $1 billion.

"When Indiegogo called us, that flipped the equation," Mr. Coleman said. "It changed the math from 'this isn't something we feel comfortable risking,' to 'let's try it!' We have some very, very passionate fans, and we think it would be cool to let them have the opportunity to invest."

Most crowdfunding investors gamble tiny sums. About a third of the investments made on Wefunder so far are for $100, the site's minimum, and 76 percent are for $500 or less, according to Nick Tommarello, Wefunder's chief executive.

Unlike shares in public companies, which can be easily sold if an investor wants out, stock in private ventures is largely illiquid. Investors who snap up a stake in a start-up they spot on Indiegogo are most likely stuck with it for many years.

And the process is more complex and expensive than traditional crowdfunding. It costs nothing to start a regular campaign on Indiegogo. The site takes a 5 percent cut of the funds raised. The people who donate typically get an early version product in question, plus various trinkets or karmic rewards.

But for equity campaigns, creators will need to spend about $7,000 on compliance and regulatory costs, Indiegogo estimates, before a campaign is permitted to go live. The site will then take a cash fee of 7 percent on any funds raised, plus an additional 2 percent in stock. Investors will pay a $7 processing fee or 2 percent of their investment, whichever is higher.

The best-known and most active site for crowdfunding projects, Kickstarter, says it is not interested in the equity market.

"The purpose of creativity is not to become an investment vehicle," said Justin Kazmark, a Kickstarter spokesman. "When creative projects escape the need to generate profit, the result is a more vibrant and diverse culture. We're more focused on a richer culture than richer investors."

Doubts Arise as Investors Flock to Crowdfunded Start-Ups

BY NATHANIEL POPPER | JAN. 24, 2017

SAN FRANCISCO — Ryan Feit left behind his lucrative career at a private equity firm to chase the dream of crowdfunding.

Mr. Feit, a 33-year-old graduate of the Wharton School of the University of Pennsylvania, went to Washington several times to lobby for a new law that allowed small-time investors to buy stock in startups — and then set up one of the first websites that list companies trying to raise money. But what Mr. Feit has seen since he set up his site, SeedInvest, has dented his enthusiasm.

Over the last two years, his company, which is based in New York, has turned away dozens of companies that wanted to raise money from investors on his site. Some of the companies had what seemed, to Mr. Feit, to be clear red flags for investors, but later showed up on other crowdfunding sites, where they have raised hundreds of thousands of dollars from unsophisticated investors.

One of the early companies he rejected was shut down by regulators — who labeled it a fraud — after it raised $5 million from investors. And Mr. Feit expects it won't be the last.

"I'm legitimately concerned that a lot of people are going to be losing money," Mr. Feit said. "Investing in start-ups is really risky, and it's very different than buying a used couch. We definitely do not think you should treat it like Craigslist."

The promise that Mr. Feit initially saw in crowdfunding arrived with the 2012 Jumpstart Our Business Start-ups, or Jobs Act. The legislation opened the door to new methods of crowdfunding, promoted as a new way to lower the regulatory barriers that have prevented companies from raising money from ordinary people. Steve Case, the founder of AOL, and even the former president, Barack Obama, have praised the law.

With the Jobs Act, companies could raise money on sites like Mr. Feit's and offer investors an actual ownership stake, with the promise of financial returns — turning crowdfunding into a much more serious business than, say, Kickstarter.

And there have been success stories. Companies that have raised money so far have included those that the Jobs Act was hoping to help — businesses far from Silicon Valley or lacking easy access to venture capital. A craft brewery in Austin, Tex., attracted $1 million from investors in just a few months, while an indoor farming start-up in Indiana has drawn over $600,000.

Yet advocates of crowdfunding, like Mr. Feit, have been expressing concern about the low levels of compliance among many of the early companies that have raised money and the bad terms the companies have offered investors.

"Even though a lot of people want to come to the party early, they may ruin the market if the market gets a reputation for being one where people don't comply with the rules," said Joan MacLeod Heminway, a law professor at the University of Tennessee. "There are certain issuers who are definitely engaging in practices that I would consider to be dangerous to a vibrant market."

Professor Heminway has been working with a company called CrowdCheck on a survey of compliance in the industry. CrowdCheck has found that almost none of the companies that have been listed so far are fully in compliance with even the basic rules set down by the Securities and Exchange Commission.

About 40 percent of all companies, for example, did not get their financial results audited or certified, as is required by the rules, CrowdCheck found. The lower regulatory barriers for crowdfunding mean that the S.E.C. does not individually check whether companies are following the requirements.

That job is left to the sites that list investments, like SeedInvest. Mr. Feit's site lists only companies that are deemed by CrowdCheck to be fully compliant. But most sites have been less choosy.

Chris Tyrrell, the chairman of a crowdfunding industry group, the Crowdfund Intermediary Regulatory Advocates, agreed that there was an "industry level risk" because crowdfunding sites are listing investments with a patina of a regulatory approval but little quality control.

"Platforms are putting unvetted offerings out into the marketplace that could have a big blowup," said Mr. Tyrrell, who is also the founder of the site OfferBoard.

He and Mr. Feit have been pushing for a set of standards that crowdfunding sites will use when vetting companies seeking to raise funds.

A spokeswoman for the S.E.C. said the agency had no comment on the level of compliance in the industry. But regulators appear to be paying some attention.

In December, the Financial Industry Regulatory Authority announced that it had shut down a Virginia-based site, uFundingPortal, that was listing potential investments without following the most basic terms of the law.

The shutdown of uFunding, though, came only after the site had been live for months, with Finra's approval, listing over a dozen investments that complied with almost none of the rules, according to CrowdCheck.

Despite problems like these, the opportunity for companies to blow up and lose money for investors, has been quite small so far. The signature element of the crowdfunding law, which allows companies to sell stock to anyone on the internet, went into effect last May, and only about 200 companies have sought out investments to date. The law caps at $1 million the amount that a single company can raise from ordinary investors.

But Congress is currently considering a change to the crowdfunding law that would make it easier for companies to raise money online.

Sherwood Neiss, the founder of Crowdfund Capital Advisors, a consulting firm, said that he was confident that the crowd had enough wisdom to screen out the bad companies and those that were not providing enough information.

As evidence for that, Mr. Neiss pointed to the dozen or so companies that tried to raise money on the uFunding site, without the disclosures required by law. None of the companies raised more than a few hundred dollars before uFunding was shut down.

But the crowd did not manage to catch the problems with Ascenergy, a company in Nevada that raised $5 million on crowdfunding sites with a promise of creating an oil and gas business. The company used a less discussed provision of the Jobs Act that allowed it to raise more than $1 million from more sophisticated investors.

When the S.E.C. shut down Ascenergy in 2015, the agency said the company did not appear to have any of the expertise or contacts in the oil industry that it had claimed in its online material.

By the time Ascenergy was stopped, the company had already spent most of the millions of dollars it collected from 90 or so investors. Much of it was used for the personal expenses of its founder, paying for "fast-food restaurants, Apple stores and iTunes, dietary supplements and personal care products," the S.E.C. said.

A lawyer for Ascenergy did not respond to a request for comment.

Mr. Feit, whose site had rejected Ascenergy, said that he was less worried about outright frauds and more concerned about companies that were unlikely to ever pay off and that were not giving investors enough information to judge them.

Mr. Feit has been particularly worried about companies that have assigned themselves sky-high valuations that will make it hard for investors to ever make their money back. In several cases, companies that he rejected because of their high valuations have shown up on other sites with the same valuations.

Mr. Feit and Mr. Tyrrell have been leading an effort through the Crowdfund Intermediary Regulatory Advocates to create a set of industry standards that all crowdfunding sites will adhere to when they vet potential investments, which will include a consideration of valuations and compliance.

Mr. Feit and Mr. Tyrrell have led two conference calls about the potential standards with other crowdfunding sites, but the site that has hosted the majority of crowdfunding campaigns so far, Wefunder, has not responded to invitations to take part.

Nick Tommarello, co-founder of Wefunder, said that his site had to be sure companies were following all the rules. But he said he did not think, as Mr. Feit does, that it is the place of crowdfunding sites like his to argue with companies over their proper value. That, he said, would defeat the purpose of crowdfunding.

"It's not my job to be a gatekeeper," he said. "It's my job to be sure everyone knows the risks they are taking and that they have all the information they need."

To help investors assess risks, Mr. Tommarello is preparing to introduce a function on Wefunder that will allow expert investors to weigh in with their analysis of companies listed on the site.

Mr. Tommarello also noted that many small-time investors so far were viewing their investments more as donations to businesses they like, rather than as investments that will make money.

Marc Leaf, a lawyer who has analyzed the early crowdfunding campaigns for the law firm Drinker Biddle, said that so far many companies were asking for investments on terms that few real venture capitalists would accept.

"I would expect them to be very risky," Mr. Leaf said. "The question is, Over time, will we see that there is a wisdom in the crowds or will we see that there is a madness in the crowds?"

Texas Lawmaker Proposes Crowdfunding to Tackle Backlog of Rape Kits

BY CHRISTINE HAUSER | MARCH 15, 2017

THOUSANDS OF RAPE investigations are bogged down in Texas because of untested evidence, but a lawmaker has proposed a bill that would use public crowdfunding to help pay for testing and fix the backlog.

In the first legislation of its kind, the lawmaker, State Representative Victoria Neave, a Democrat from Dallas, introduced the bill in February to solicit donations of $1 or more from people when they renew or apply for driver's licenses. The money would underwrite a grant for the Department of Public Safety to test what are commonly called "rape kits," which consist of evidence samples including hair, semen, fabric fibers and skin cells.

"It was an issue that we thought was really important," Ms. Neave said in an interview on Tuesday. "We know that women don't always get to the point of reporting the incident, and when they have the courage to voluntarily undergo the test, that takes a lot of courage.

"My view is that the least thing we can do is make sure that these kits get tested," she said. "We owe it to them."

The bill had its first public hearing in the state's capital on Monday. A final vote would take place before the legislative session ends in May.

If adopted, it could generate an estimated $1 million a year, based on similar donations collected for veterans from driver's license applications, according to a legislative budget document. When administrative costs are deducted, that would leave more than $800,000 every fiscal year that local governments could tap to push through testing of evidence collected from the victims of sexual assault during a physical examination that can take four to six hours.

The donations are intended to supplement rather than replace a budget for the testing, which can cost $1,000 to $1,500 for each kit. The Legislature, which is now in budget talks, is also considering allocating $4 million to fund the process, said Rebecca Acuna, Ms. Neave's chief of staff.

Like other states, Texas has been struggling for years to work through its backlog of untested evidence samples, which are examined for DNA to help law enforcement officials identify a suspect.

The state is not alone in trying to put a dent in the backlog of rape kits with crowdfunding and other unique approaches. In 2014, in what was seen as a model for jurisdictions around the country, the Manhattan district attorney's office in New York announced a program to use $35 million in civil forfeiture assets to help other cities and states tackle their own backlogs.

That one-time funding has helped testing proceed in other states, including Pennsylvania, the state's auditor, Eugene DePasquale, wrote in a blog post in January.

In Detroit, after more than 11,000 rape kits were discovered in 2009 in a Police Department storage facility, the Michigan Women's Foundation, the Detroit Crime Commission and the Wayne County prosecutor's office teamed up in a fund-raising effort called Enough SAID.

The group has since raised money to test more than 10,000 kits, it said on its website.

But enshrining the crowdfunding with state law is still relatively new. In New Mexico, State Representative Bealquin Gomez sponsored a bill, similar to the Texas proposal, that has passed the House vote and is headed to the Senate. It calls for a mechanism enabling people to donate through their tax returns, he said in an interview.

A similar bill is pending in California, said Ilse Knecht, the policy and advocacy director for the Joyful Heart Foundation, a national organization that advocates for victims of sexual assault, domestic violence and child abuse, and runs the testing initiative End the Backlog.

The foundation said in a statement on its website that it estimates there are hundreds of thousands of untested kits in police and crime lab storage facilities throughout the country.

Over the years, Texas has tried to chip away at its untested evidence kits. In 2013, $11 million was set aside in budget funds to test kits that had gone unexamined between 1996 and 2011, Department of Public Safety figures show. By the end of January of this year, 8,741 kits from that period had been tested, but 3,604 have not yet been handled, Tom Vinger, a department spokesman, said in an email.

Thousands more untested kits have accumulated since 2011.

Christopher Kaiser, the public policy director at the Texas Association Against Sexual Assault, a victims advocacy group, said the bill was only a partial fix.

"I certainly understand where it is coming from, but I will say that I don't think private donations should be seen as taking the place of the state's duty to fund this work," he said. "But we support the bill."

There is no federal law that mandates the tracking and testing of rape kits.

In many states, the untested kits have built up over the years, mostly because of budget and staffing constraints, according to End the Backlog. Sometimes a test is set aside because the rapist has been identified or is already in jail.

But forensic analysts and advocates say testing the kits should be pursued anyway, because it can also identify serial rapists or lead to exonerations.

Mr. Kaiser said some cases are not an investigative priority, such as if the victim and the perpetrator knew each other or if questions arise about consent.

"What got us here in the first place is gender bias," Mr. Kaiser said. "It is unlike the relationship of the perpetrator to the victim in other crimes. I do think there is a unique aspect to this when we are talking about sexual violence and why we are even in this backlog situation in the first place."

Utah Paleontologists Turn to Crowdfunding for Raptor Project

BY ASHER ELBEIN | AUG. 28, 2017

MILLIONS OF YEARS AGO, on a mud flat somewhere in Cretaceous Utah, a group of Utahraptors made a grave mistake: They tried to hunt near quicksand. The pack's poor fortune has given modern paleontologists an opportunity to decode the giant raptor — its appearance, growth and behavior — but only if they can raise the money.

Enter "The Utahraptor Project," started on GoFundMe last year with a $100,000 goal. It offers backers access to a field worker's blog, a live "Raptor Cam" and digital models of the find put together through the process of photogrammetry. While it is far from reaching its goal, the team is optimistic.

"Once we get this up and running, with all the cameras and gizmos to record the action on a micro and macro level," said Scott Madsen, a fossil preparator, "I think we can give the public a good show for their money."

Utahraptor, 23 feet long and weighing over a ton, was one of the largest dromaeosaurs, feathered, sickle-clawed dinosaurs closely related to birds. Since its discovery in 1991, it has been the subject of a popular novel, assorted documentaries and tie-in toys from "Jurassic Park." But for all its fame, the predator has been known primarily from only a few remains. That changed in 2001, when a geology student found a leg bone emerging from a hillside in the Cedar Mountain formation in eastern Utah.

Over 12 field seasons, a team of paleontologists with the Utah Geological Survey found an ever-expanding tangle of bones in the 126-million-year-old rock. When the final slab of sandstone was removed in 2014, said Jim Kirkland, Utah state paleontologist, it weighed nine tons and contained the skeletons of a herbivorous dinosaur, a 16-foot adult Utahraptor, four juveniles and a recent hatchling.

The block proved too heavy for the lab at the University of Utah, and in 2015 ended up on reinforced floors at the Museum of Ancient Life at Thanksgiving Point. Mr. Madsen, then an employee of the Utah Geological Survey with experience preparing fossils at Dinosaur National Monument, began the long process of cleaning the bones. Two months later, he had been laid off: The agency's budget, which is partly funded by the proceeds from drilling on state land, was hit hard by the 2014 plunge in oil prices. There wasn't any money to pay him.

Without Mr. Madsen, the Utahraptor block sat in limbo. Attempts to find outside funding didn't go well, Dr. Kirkland said: The Museum of Ancient Life declined to help raise money for the block over concerns it would conflict with the museum's own fund-raising efforts. With attempts to get corporate sponsors coming to nothing, Mr. Madsen suggested a crowdfunding campaign to pay for the setup and hours of labor needed to properly document the fossils.

Paleontologists have turned to crowdfunding before, though usually only for a few thousand dollars at most, Mr. Madsen said. The size of the block required a more ambitious funding push.

The Utahraptor Project has attracted interest from dinosaur enthusiasts on social media and paleontology blogs. But while donations ranging from $5 to $1,500 have trickled in, the campaign has raised only $15,150 over the past 10 months. That is enough to buy some basic tools and begin work, Mr. Madsen said, but not enough for the team's more ambitious goals.

Mr. Madsen has yet to be paid for his efforts. "I'm in a personally awkward place doing this crowdfunding thing, not least of which because I'm asking for money to pay myself for this work."

The contents of the block already offer some intriguing possibilities, Dr. Kirkland said. They represent the remains of predators that stumbled into quicksand while pursuing trapped prey, one of the first such cases in the fossil record. Dr. Kirkland wants to determine whether each of the seven animals arrived at different times, or whether a single pack was buried at once. If the bones are interlaced, or show signs of equivalent amounts of weathering, that would be good evidence for a rich family life for Utahraptor.

The exposed bones also suggest that Utahraptor looked quite different from previous projections. While the juveniles are long and lanky in the classic raptor mold, the adult appears to have packed on mass to deal with bigger prey. "The front end of the jaw is unlike any other meat-eating dinosaur I've ever seen," Dr. Kirkland said. "It's not just a blown-up Velociraptor. This thing is built like Arnold Schwarzenegger. Or a Sherman tank."

Other paleontologists are watching the project with interest. "We already know there are many bones in this block which fill in the anatomy of Utahraptor, but there are probably plenty more surprises in there," said Tom Holtz, a University of Maryland paleontologist specializing in predatory dinosaurs. "We won't know until the lab has worked its way through the rock."

Future plans for the campaign include a panel at the Salt Lake Comic Con next month, said B. J. Nicholls, the social media coordinator for the project. Organizers hope the publicity will help drive donations; the search for corporate sponsors continues as well. For Dr. Kirkland, Utahraptor is part of his legacy: he named the species and has long been associated with it. For years, he has dreamed of a state park with the Utahraptor block as its centerpiece. But he will settle for making sure the find is treated properly before he retires.

"We can't do this over again," he said. "We may never find another site like this. I'd rather let it sit than not do it with the very best data collection and the finest preparators we can have work on it."

"We worked to get this block down the hill for 10 years," he added. "We can't screw it up."

CHAPTER 2

Supporting the Arts and Entertainment

Projects in the arts and entertainment are common crowdfunding campaigns, particularly when they can appeal to a large existing fan base. The entirely fan-backed "Veronica Mars" reunion film, which broke several fund-raising records in 2012 by raising $2 million in only eleven hours, demonstrated what a community of passionate fans can accomplish. Albums, plays, art exhibitions, video games and even the restoration of aging paintings are all examples of successful campaigns in the arts. This chapter illustrates several examples of community-funded arts projects.

'Veronica Mars' Fans Are Happy to Finance a Reunion

BY DAVE ITZKOFF | MARCH 5, 2014

LOS ANGELES — Hardly a week after Cyrus and Ina Chung had moved to Providence, R.I., to start new jobs, this married couple were standing here in a parking lot, dressed in formal clothes with the Southern California sun bearing down on them in late June, having paid a total of $3,000 for the privilege of being extras in the "Veronica Mars" movie.

Mr. Chung, a lawyer and devoted viewer of the cult television series of the same name, which starred Kristen Bell as a sarcastic teenage detective, still recalled the day that previous March when Ms. Bell and Rob Thomas, the "Veronica Mars" creator, announced that they were seeking donations to raise the film's budget on Kickstarter, the online crowdfunding site.

After discovering that many tantalizing rewards promised to top donors had already been claimed, Mr. Chung moved quickly when two nonspeaking background roles became available.

"I think this is the most excited I've ever seen him," Ms. Chung said on the set. "Even more than our wedding."

Now, nearly a year after some 91,000 donors contributed about $5.7 million to revive "Veronica Mars" after it was canceled in 2007, and months after a whirlwind 24-day film shoot, this much-discussed movie will be released March 14 in theaters and via video on demand.

After one of the first celebrity Kickstarter campaigns, the arrival of the "Veronica Mars" movie raises mysteries that even its titular crime solver — now a law-school graduate who is drawn into a murder case in her hometown — would find challenging.

What would success look like for "Veronica Mars"? Will it set off a stampede of studios reviving dormant franchises in crowdfunded projects, or was it a one-time phenomenon? Will it even work as a movie, and will anyone other than its most obsessive fans want to see it?

"This is new to me," Mr. Thomas said from his trailer earlier that morning, "and a lot of it is outside my comfort zone."

When CW canceled "Veronica Mars" after its third season, Mr. Thomas said, he intentionally gave the series an unsatisfying resolution, hoping the network might pause before pulling the plug.

"They told me at the time, 'Hey, there's a chance you won't be back, if you want to tie things up nicely,' " recalled Mr. Thomas, a former college football player who has retained his muscular build. "And my view was, 'No, I don't want to make it easy for you to cancel us.' "

For the next five years, Mr. Thomas, whose other shows have included short-lived cult hits like "Party Down," said he could not complete an interview without being asked when the show — which had never drawn much more than three million viewers an episode — would be turned into a movie.

While Warner Bros., which owns “Veronica Mars,” was willing to consider a direct-to-video sequel, Mr. Thomas said he had no interest in such a project, and the studio’s marketing surveys, he said, did not show enough nationwide familiarity with the property to warrant a multimillion-dollar investment for a proper feature film.

“At that time, I thought we were dead,” he said.

That changed as Mr. Thomas took note of websites like Kickstarter, which held the potential to convert the fervent enthusiasm of a modest audience into needed dollars for a lower-budget movie. To that point, the site was a launching pad for offbeat inventions and grass-roots efforts — Mr. Thomas had used it to give money to the indie rock band Cotton Mather for an album rerelease — and a route to Hollywood, rather than a mechanism Hollywood could make use of.

But in 2012, when Mr. Thomas and Ms. Bell were preparing to post an online video that would announce this fund-raising drive, Mr. Thomas said, Warner Bros. denied them permission to do so.

“It was as hopeless as I’ve ever felt,” said Mr. Thomas, who considered releasing the video anyway, then thought better of it.

What he said was as important as the money that could be generated was “the heat that comes by being the first one out of the gate,” which would make a “Veronica Mars” film “the ‘Blair Witch Project’ of crowdfunded movies.”

“It petrified me for a year,” Mr. Thomas said. “I kept thinking, ‘I’m going to wake up tomorrow and someone else is going to be doing this.’ ”

Thomas Gewecke, the chief digital officer at Warner Bros. Entertainment, said in an interview that this was not a false start on the part of the studio.

Mr. Gewecke said Warner Bros. wanted the Kickstarter campaign “to be as successful as it could possibly be,” and “wanted to make sure it was set up to have the maximum chance of success.”

“Rob and Kristen had a very well-developed, clearly articulated vision,” he said. “Their relationship with the fans was strong, and the fan base was incredibly passionate.”

When Mr. Thomas and Ms. Bell's pitch went live last year, with a goal of garnering $2 million in a month, it hit that target in less than 12 hours and went on to nearly triple that in 30 days. (Prizes and incentives offered to donors, like autographed posters and voice mail messages from Ms. Bell, surely helped, as did a tidal wave of news media coverage.)

Ms. Bell, who was speaking from the "Veronica Mars" set three months after giving birth to her daughter, Lincoln, said she was deeply concerned that the crowdfunding drive would be a judgment on her clout to carry a film.

"There was a moment when I thought, 'Could this be a direct reflection of whether or not I'm wanted as an actress at all?' " said Ms. Bell, whose résumé includes films like "Forgetting Sarah Marshall" and the Showtime series "House of Lies."

"It's a thumbs-up or thumbs-down, right in your face," she said. (Had the "Veronica Mars" film not happened, she said, "I would have just spent the summer with the baby.")

Still, Ms. Bell said there was something special about the Veronica Mars character, who is sharp-tongued and unconcerned about fitting in with the in-crowd, that longtime fans would want to support.

"Rob wrote Veronica as this queen of the disenfranchised," Ms. Bell said. "All these people who were affected by Veronica, who say, 'This got me through high school,' were able to say: 'I now have a job. I can give you 10 bucks.' "

Many of the several dozen backers on the "Veronica Mars" set in June seemed to agree with Ms. Bell's assessment, though they had paid upward of $2,500 to play additional guests at the character's high-school reunion.

These donors, mostly in their 20s and 30s, had watched the series in its original run or discovered it on video, and spoke of their eagerness to see the story continue. They understood that they were not investors in the movie and would not receive any potential profits, and that their contributions only covered part of its budget.

(Warner Bros., which is paying for fulfillment costs like the delivery of "Veronica Mars" DVDs and T-shirts, declined to say how much more it had chipped in.)

Andrea Cremer, a Kickstarter backer and author of the "Nightshade" young-adult novels, said she had contributed $2,500 because she wanted to see if Veronica would reunite with her sometime boyfriend Logan Echolls (played by Jason Dohring).

"It's a big chunk of money," Ms. Cremer said. "I was planning on going on vacation this summer, and it was like, well, either vacation budget or 'Veronica Mars.' "

Steven Dengler, a Toronto entrepreneur and a founder of the currency website xe.com, said he gave $10,000 to "Veronica Mars" because it had made Kickstarter "a benchmark, opened it up to a wider audience and made it a household term."

The financial success of the "Veronica Mars" campaign opened the floodgates on the celebrity sales pitches and vanity projects that have become ubiquitous on the site: a movie directed by Zach Braff that received additional funding from an independent studio even though it met its $2 million target; a proposed romantic comedy from Melissa Joan Hart that failed to reach its $2 million goal. But Mr. Dengler said Kickstarter users could tell which proposals were fully thought out and worthy of their donations.

In cases like "Veronica Mars," he said, "People have said: 'Yes, I would like resolution. I would like to see those characters come back and explore what happened to them later on.' That's accessible, and that's something you can sell."

"Other people have said: 'Hi, I'm someone famous that you know. Give me money to make something,' " he added. "And it's like: 'You know what? No.' It doesn't have the same sort of resonance."

Still, Warner Bros. was coy about discussing box office expectations for "Veronica Mars" (which will play in only about 270 theaters to start), or detailing how much it hoped to make from sales of tickets and digital downloads.

Mr. Gewecke would only say, "We definitely already view this as a big success."

Nor would the studio say what its further plans were for "Veronica Mars," whether as a continuing franchise of high- or low-budget movies or in some other format, or what other titles in its library it might similarly resuscitate.

"We are always looking at: Are there other properties that make sense?" Mr. Gewecke said. "Are there other new ways of thinking about how we bring titles to market?"

He added: "We look at every opportunity, case by case. We're really pleased with how this has turned out."

Mr. Thomas said he believed Warner Bros. was taking the right approach with "Veronica Mars," given the size and scope of the film.

"It would scare the hell out of me if they decided, 'Hey, we're going to put $30 million in publicity behind it and release it on 3,000 screens,' " he said.

"If we made back our money and then some, that would be thrilling," Mr. Thomas said. "I don't expect to compete with the 'Twilight' movies."

In the eyes of Kickstarter donors like Kari Sutherland, a senior editor of children's books at HarperCollins who was 27 weeks pregnant when she visited the "Veronica Mars" shoot, there is no way the film can fall short of their fantasies.

Recalling a conversation she had with her husband, a neuropsychologist, before she came to the set, Ms. Sutherland said he told her, " 'You know it's going to get made, Kari.' I was like: 'Yes, this is true. And we're going to see it multiple times.' "

When he asked, " 'We are?' ," she answered, " 'Yes, we are.' "

Soliciting Funds From the Crowd? Results Will Vary

BY ELIZABETH OLSON | MARCH 19, 2014

ESTABLISHED MUSEUMS LIKE the Smithsonian Institution are increasingly turning to crowdfunding appeals to help pay for exhibits and programs that tight budgets might otherwise preclude.

Individual artists have been soliciting donations from the public for years, using Internet fund-raising platforms like Kickstarter, Indiegogo and Razoo to defray the costs of producing their work. Museums, long reliant on corporate sponsorships, gifts and bequests, have been more hesitant to raise funds digitally because the substantial commitment of staff time required for such campaigns does not always produce a big financial win.

But the successes of some of the museum world's biggest institutions is spurring interest by museum fund-raisers. The Louvre, for example, used crowdfunding — the solicitation of money from individuals online — to raise more than $1 million two years ago to purchase two 13th-century ivory figurines.

Other big-name museums have had smaller successes. The Phillips Collection in Washington surpassed its $15,000 goal last year on Indiegogo to finance a room sculpted from beeswax by the German artist Wolfgang Laib, and the Arthur A. Sackler Gallery, part of the Smithsonian, raised $176,000 to defray some costs of an exhibit on art connected with yoga.

"The Smithsonian effort was the biggest campaign undertaken by an American museum," said Laura Kakolewski, marketing manager for Americans for the Arts, an organization that promotes museums. "Museums are taking a cue from artists and tapping into a new potential source of donors, and creating a sense of belonging among their patrons."

Such campaigns require resources and staff time to design the visual and other elements including the website, oversee the email and social media contacts, and follow up with efforts to convert new givers to loyal, longtime donors. And if a campaign misfires and does not attract public money, the failure is visibly embarrassing.

The Smithsonian had some bad luck with online fund-raising. When its Hirshhorn Museum sought to raise $35,000 on Causes.com to bring a sculpture by the Chinese dissident Ai Weiwei to Washington in 2012, the effort raised only $555, the website showed. The same year, the Smithsonian's American Art Museum raised only a few thousand dollars for an exhibit to be called "Art of Video Games." Participants could donate $10 online to play a video game on the museum's website.

With the yoga exhibit, the Smithsonian took another chance on digital fund-raising because it was a "perfect meeting point of a popular practice that people are invested in, and the limited resources we had to carry out the exhibit," said Yoonhyung Lee, the institution's director of digital media philanthropy.

Since yoga has millions of devoted practitioners, she said, the museum felt it would more easily attract backers. The money raised was spent on shipping art from England and India, publishing a color catalog and hosting free public programs. While the exhibit had been planned far in advance to borrow 130 sculptures and other objects from 25 museums around the world, the Sackler did not have the funds for the additional events.

Other appeals that have attracted substantial support include the effort by the Architecture and Design Museum in Los Angeles, which last month surpassed its $40,000 goal, from 436 backers, on Kickstarter for the "Never Built" exhibition, which will show how differently the city would look if certain projects had been constructed.

Kickstarter, which has 135 appeals tagged as museum projects on its website, also hosted an effort to create the Marina Abramovic Institute, which is devoted to performance art. The appeal raised $661,452 in August, attracting nearly 5,000 supporters to the project.

But there have been notable failures, too. The Philip J. Curie Dinosaur Museum, in Grand Prairie, Alberta, tried to raise $1 million on Indiegogo to help construct a new museum, but raised only $34,000. The project went ahead anyway with more traditional sources of financing and government grants.

A Kickstarter campaign last year to raise $9,900 to clean and preserve Thomas Allen's painting "Evening Market" by the Hunter Museum of American Art in Chattanooga, Tenn., collected only $3,371. On Kickstarter, failure to reach the goal means the project gets no money.

To help museums mount successful campaigns, the American Alliance of Museums offers a web seminar and the fund-raising platforms, which make money by taking a percentage of the funds raised, offer online videos, guidance and some coaching.

Another impetus to try such alternative fund-raising is research that shows online giving is rising, with donations to arts and culture increasing 8.5 percent last year, said Steve MacLaughlin, of Blackbaud, a software provider for nonprofits.

"The total percentage of arts and culture giving that comes from online sources is 6.8 percent — a percentage which is greater than the 6.4 percent for overall online giving sources," he said.

Ms. Lee, of the Smithsonian, said: "Everyone wants to do it, but the amount of work involved is enormous, whether it's to raise $10,000 or $100,000."

Allison Peck, the head of marketing and public affairs for the Sackler and the Freer Gallery of Art, also part of the Smithsonian, who worked on the "Together We Are One" yoga exhibit effort, said, "It takes a lot of time, and you have to create a buzz around it." The exhibit, which is traveling to other cities, is now at San Francisco's Asian Art Museum.

Ms. Peck and her colleagues started their effort six weeks before the May 2013 start of the campaign, deciding on its goals, hiring a contractor to create a campaign video and creating a website, printable posters and an array of social media tools.

To spark interest, they enlisted yoga messengers, a group of yoga teachers and practitioners, through local contacts. About 250 such messengers either distributed materials or held yoga classes to acquaint people with the fund-raising effort.

The Smithsonian also constructed a detailed chart with a daily message schedule on the Internet and a weekly theme, such as yoga and health, with information presented on a one-minute video, blog and email message. Communications with potential givers were coordinated with planned giving by sponsors to ask for matching gifts.

Lesley Mansford, chief executive of Razoo, which hosted the Smithsonian campaign, said each fund-raising effort needed to be small and targeted, and supported by donors and social media influencers.

"It's not just putting a page up on the Internet and hoping people will come," she said.

The Smithsonian campaigners also followed up with thank-you emails and tax receipts, and, as a reward, inscribed the names of donors on a digital plaque they created.

A big chunk of the Smithsonian's fund-raising take came from its corporate sponsor Whole Foods, which gave $70,000. An anonymous corporate giver provided $30,000, leaving the donations from the public at around $76,000, the Smithsonian said.

While that is still substantial, Ms. Lee said the Smithsonian would be cautious about future initiatives. Digital giving, she predicted, was "unlikely to replace traditional giving. It's like trying to fill a bucket with one grain of sand."

Neil Young's Digital Music Project Raises $6.2 Million Online

BY BEN SISARIO | APRIL 15, 2014

PONOMUSIC, THE HIGH-DEFINITION digital audio business from Neil Young, has raised $6.2 million on Kickstarter, making it that crowdfunding platform's third-most successful project.

The Pono project, which includes a portable player as well as an online store for music, is the culmination of years of hopes by Mr. Young to correct what he views as the poor audio quality available to most consumers, first on CDs and then on MP3s and other digital formats. The triangular-shaped Pono device, designed in conjunction with the audio company Ayre Acoustics, will play high-quality digital files sold through Pono's store, where albums are expected to cost from $15 to $25.

The Kickstarter page for Pono — named after a Hawaiian word meaning goodness or righteousness — went online a month ago, and blew past its stated fund-raising goal of $800,000 within the first 10 hours. After one full day it had raised $1.6 million, and contributions continued steadily as the company added special "artist signature editions" of the $400 player from Metallica, ZZ Top, the Eagles, Norah Jones, Pearl Jam, Arcade Fire and other music stars.

When the campaign ended on Tuesday afternoon, it had raised a total of $6,223,754 from 18,220 individual backers. Ninety-six of those people pledged $5,000 or more for the top premium, which included attendance at one of four V.I.P. dinners and listening parties with Mr. Young, 68. The devices are expected to be shipped to customers in October.

The most-funded projects in Kickstarter's four-year history are the Pebble smart watch, which raised $10.3 million, and the OUYA video game console, which raised $8.6 million, both in 2012. The "Veronica Mars" movie project drew $5.7 million last year, and led to the film's release last month, featuring some pledging fans as extras.

Smell of the Greasepaint, the Funds of the Crowd

BY PATRICK HEALY | JULY 27, 2014

LONDON — As an up-and-coming theater producer, Jamie Hendry didn't have many investors when he started raising money for a musical based on the children's novel "The Wind in the Willows."

What his show did have was a famous title and a celebrity script writer, Julian Fellowes, the creator of "Downton Abbey." And their publicity value came in handy given how Mr. Hendry was trying to raise money for the show here: by appealing to the masses.

He raised about one million pounds ($1.7 million) last winter by selling equity stakes in "Willows" in relatively small units of £1,000, £2,500 and £5,000 through an online campaign. Any British citizen could buy in with a debit card by visiting Mr. Hendry's website, which included a plainly worded prospectus dotted with images of Toad and Mole, characters from the story. He had the money in three months from 400 people, and he now has a list of 10,000 others who signed up to learn about investing in the future. "Willows" hopes to open in the West End in the fall of 2015.

Call it entrepreneurship or gimmickry, but Mr. Hendry's strategy was London theater's most ambitious attempt at crowdfunding — and a method that will soon become an option for New York producers. Proposed changes to United States securities rules, which could take effect by this fall, will make it far easier for Americans to raise money the way Mr. Hendry did.

"The old-time producers with wealthy investors are a dying breed," said Mr. Hendry, who is 29 and studied computer science and management in college. "Who's going to put millions of pounds into a commercial musical when those people are no longer with us? We have to find ways to expand support for theater."

Under the proposed United States rules, theater artists and producers would be able to publicize and sell equity stakes in plays and musicals online, which is now generally prohibited. The proposed rules would also expand the pool of potential backers.

Current rules make it cumbersome to enlist so-called nonaccredited investors, or people who earn less than $200,000 a year or have a low net worth: those who might be risking their life savings on a play or musical, say, given that 75 percent of Broadway shows flop. The proposed rules would make it easier for them to invest limited sums and allow Broadway and Off Broadway productions to raise up to $1 million a year through crowdfunding websites registered with the Securities and Exchange Commission.

Under the current system, most producers have long made private equity offerings to wealthy associates and friends, many of whom have invested in theater before. Broadway plays regularly cost $3 million to produce, and musicals tend to cost $8 million or more, and investors usually put up at least $25,000 apiece; the amounts are considerably less for Off Broadway. (The equivalent amounts in London are often one-third of Broadway's numbers.)

"In American theater, we now have a powerful club of producers who work with wealthy investors to put on shows they like, and younger people don't have access," said Crystal Skillman, a New York playwright who has earned strong reviews for Off Off Broadway plays like "Geek!" and "Cut." "Being able to recruit our own investors online could become revolutionary."

Ms. Skillman and her husband, the comic book writer Fred Van Lente, are among the thousands of theater artists in the United States and Britain who have increasingly turned to crowdfunding websites like Kickstarter and Indiegogo for financing. But people donate though these platforms; they are not purchasing equity in shows.

Ms. Skillman said that she and Mr. Van Lente planned to look into selling equity in shows once the proposed securities rules take effect.

Broadway has had only one major attempt at crowdfunding: the 2011 revival of "Godspell," in which 700 people invested $1,000 or more and made up about 55 percent of the show's $5 million budget. The "Godspell" strategy was hamstrung, however, by the securities rules: Ken Davenport, the lead producer, said he could not make online sales as Mr. Hendry did, and recruiting nonaccredited investors involved red tape and legal expenses.

"I would crowdfund again, if it was the right show — 'Godspell' was about community, and we had a community of investors — and if the rules do become lighter," said Mr. Davenport, who is going the traditional route of recruiting accredited investors as a lead producer for the Broadway show "It's Only a Play" this fall.

"I just find it ridiculous in this country that we prevent people from investing in Broadway if they are not accredited and well connected to producers, and yet anyone can travel within 60 miles of their homes and bet their life savings at a casino," added Mr. Davenport, who writes a blog called The Producer's Perspective.

The "Godspell" approach has not caught on, because most Broadway producers look down on crowdfunding, citing the presence of their pools of experienced investors and the administrative headaches that Mr. Davenport had. But "Willows" could emerge as a new model, especially for Off Broadway as well as London. The producers of the current West End revival of "The Pajama Game" raised about $340,000 late last winter from 218 investors through the equity crowdfunding site Seedrs; the money accounted for 15 percent of the show's capitalization. The limited-run production is scheduled to end in September and will probably close at a loss, although the producers declined to confirm that.

Other British producers are interested in licensing Mr. Hendry's online platform, he said; he declined to name them. But several London producers said crowdfunding seemed like a tool for producers who needed cash or a stunt to raise the profile of younger ones like Mr. Hendry, who has also been a producer here on the Beatles' tribute show "Let It Be" and the musical "Legally Blonde."

"Jamie gave a very posh workshop of the musical at the Savoy Hotel, but it remains to be seen if his approach will work and if the show will indeed open," said Michael Codron, a producer who has been mounting shows here and on Broadway for more than 50 years.

"When I started out, I had a group of people — agents, other producers, people I got from my accountant — who regularly invested with me, and I was sufficiently autocratic that I didn't have to listen to their opinions," said Mr. Codron, who was responsible for major premieres of works by Tom Stoppard, David Hare and Harold Pinter, among others. "Now, I usually take a deep breath and write my own check to get shows on, because there's too much paperwork with investors today. Crowdfunding sounds like even more bureaucracy."

Mr. Hendry said he had raised "a significant chunk" of his $11 million show budget, chiefly from traditional investors, including some in the United States. As for his online investors, most of them are affluent or middle-class professionals in their 40s, 50s and 60s from London and surrounding counties, and 91 percent of them had never invested in theater before, according to a survey by Mr. Hendry's office.

"The game is on in London and New York to find the investors of the future," he said.

Crowdfunding a $500 Million Ferris Wheel, With a Wall Street Spin

BY RANDALL SMITH | SEPT. 7, 2015

INVESTING IN STOCKS is at times compared to a thrill ride — a rocket ship taking off, or a roller coaster rushing down.

The comparison may be more apt than usual for a new investment — a 630-foot Ferris wheel under construction on Staten Island — that soon will be marketed via a Wall Street version of crowdfunding.

Project leaders of the New York Wheel, which has already raised around $450 million in equity and debt, plan to seek another $30 million through North Capital Private Securities, a Utah broker-dealer that intends to sell some of the new shares via its 99Funding online crowdfunding platform and other crowdfunding sites.

Crowdfunding on websites like Kickstarter has allowed people and organizations to raise money for various projects from supporters who don't have any formal economic interest in the ventures.

Numerous online venues, often in partnership with smaller and midsize securities firms such as North Capital, have adopted provisions of the Jumpstart Our Business Startups Act of 2012, or JOBS Act, which loosened restrictions on stock sales by business start-ups.

Jim Dowd, founder and chief executive of North Capital, said he believed that the $500 million New York Wheel project "is going to be the largest transaction we're aware of that has crowdfunding."

The sale of these new shares is possible under a JOBS Act provision that went into effect in 2013, allowing private stock sales to "accredited" wealthy investors who meet certain income or networth tests.

While some of the shares will be sold conventionally by brokers, Mr. Dowd said, other shares will be sold through 99Funding to "self-directed investors," those who sign up on their own. He said the offering was planned for a 90-day period before the year's end.

The New York Wheel was originally backed by a group of wealthy investors including the real estate moguls Jeffrey Feil and Lloyd Goldman and the Jordache jeans magnate Joseph Nakash, according to Rich Marin, the project's chief executive. A sprawling outlet mall is also planned nearby.

Mr. Marin and Mr. Dowd are longtime business associates who both previously worked at Bear Stearns and Bankers Trust. North Capital plans to add up to a dozen other crowdfunding sites to participate in the fund-raising, and expects to set a minimum investment size of $5,000 to $10,000, Mr. Dowd added.

Construction on the wheel began in May, after the project raised $195 million in senior debt from the Highbridge Capital Management hedge fund unit of JPMorgan Chase, and $150 million in additional debt from CanAm Enterprises, under an American program that allows foreign nationals — CanAm investors, in this case — to gain legal residency in the United States by making job-creating investments. Another $24 million is due next month from the CanAm investors.

One sign of risk associated with the project is that the Highbridge debt carries an interest rate of 10.25 percent. But the CanAm interest rate is just 2.75 percent.

An earlier effort at selling stock to round out financing for the wheel — which began last fall by another securities firm, Houlihan Lokey — raised $31 million, falling about $15 million short of its target, Mr. Marin said. The project's original backers invested about $80 million, he added. The Houlihan sale was cut short by the New York Wheel project leaders, who needed to close other components of the financing — curtailing Houlihan's time to try to raise the remaining funds.

The ability of start-ups to raise money via crowdfunding is expected to expand further once securities regulators complete the rules under another part of the JOBS Act that will allow businesses to raise funds from accredited and unaccredited investors.

Dara Albright, a crowd-finance expert who co-founded the LendIt and FinFair conferences on alternative finance, cautions investors not to lose sight of the inherent risks in such ventures, especially since these investors don't typically get the same amount of information about sales, profits and other business metrics that public companies are required to disclose. "These things are risky," she said.

With Help From Kickstarter, Chicago Gets a Museum That Relishes the Hot Dog

BY MATT BEARDMORE | SEPT. 18, 2015

FOODSEUM OPENS ITS first exhibition, "The Hot Dog and Encased Meat of the World," on Saturday at Block 37 in Chicago's Loop; it runs through Dec. 20.

The free pop-up food museum was financed through a Kickstarter campaign last year that raised more than $33,000.

"Because we are a Chicago-based organization, we wanted to do something as a tribute to our city," said Kyle Joseph, the executive director of Foodseum. "The hot dog is very core to the city."

The interactive exhibit, which Mr. Joseph said was designed to "inspire people and open people's minds to the foods we eat," will have three major components: the history of hot dogs and encased meats, international flavors (including a smell station), and farm to fork, which will showcase the steps needed to make the meats.

Foodseum will be open Wednesday through Sunday from 11 a.m. to 7 p.m.

It is not the only museum news in the city.

From Oct. 1 to 7, the 11 museums and one zoo located on Chicago Park District property will offer visitors a number of special programs, events and exclusive deals as part of the first Chicago Museum Week. The participating institutions include the Adler Planetarium, Art Institute of Chicago, Chicago History Museum, DuSable Museum of African American History, Field Museum of Natural History, Shedd Aquarium, Lincoln Park Zoo, Museum of Contemporary Art, Museum of Science and Industry, National Museum of Mexican Art, National Museum of Puerto Rican Arts & Culture, and the Peggy Notebaert Nature Museum.

“We already work together as a loose coalition,” said Marc Miller, co-chair of the marketing committee of Museums in the Park and vice president of external affairs at the Peggy Notebaert Nature Museum. “We were talking about it in our marketing group that everyone else has a week, so why can’t we celebrate our own cultural institutions and destinations and help people get reconnected with the arts and culture?”

Kickstarter as a Path to Grammy Nominations, Far Beyond the Indie Scene

BY BEN SISARIO | FEB. 2, 2016

THREE YEARS AGO, the Nashville Symphony was in austerity mode as it recovered from the financial crisis and a flood that caused $40 million in damage to its building. To help finance an album of works by the composer Joan Tower, the orchestra turned for the first time to a source more associated with indie rock than with classical music: Kickstarter.

The orchestra's campaign raised $15,585 from 86 backers, and this month, "Stroke," one of Ms. Tower's pieces from the resulting album, is up for a Grammy Award for best contemporary classical composition.

RICHARD PERRY/THE NEW YORK TIMES

Molly Neuman, a veteran of the indie music scene who is Kickstarter's head of music, at the company's headquarters in Brooklyn.

"This project could not have happened were it not for the Kickstarter campaign," said Alan D. Valentine, president of the Nashville Symphony.

Once viewed as a fringe area where baby bands make earnest pleas for help, Kickstarter and other crowdfunding sites like it have become part of the standard financial circuit for musicians of all types, with releases that are edging closer to the mainstream. This year, four albums connected to Kickstarter campaigns are up for Grammy Awards; in previous years, four have won.

Since its founding in 2009, Kickstarter — where artists, inventors and other creative types solicit early payments from supporters — has raised $1.9 billion for nearly 100,000 projects of various kinds. Music has been the most popular category, with 22,000 successful campaigns that have raised $149 million, although creators in areas like technology and film have raised larger sums for fewer projects. (Kickstarter campaigns are completed, and supporters charged, only if pledges reach a minimum level set by the artist.) Amanda Palmer holds the record for the most money raised for a music project, $1.2 million for her 2012 album, "Theatre Is Evil."

At any given time, around 500 music-related campaigns are underway on Kickstarter, and a scan shows plenty that fit the site's stereotype of indie strivers in boho capitals: a solo ukulele album from a performer in Seattle, a Brooklyn band working on its first live release.

But the Grammy nominations this year also show the site's breadth. The composer Andrew Norman's "Play" is also up for contemporary composition, on an album by the Boston Modern Orchestra Project; Miguel Zenón's "Identities Are Changeable" has a nod for best Latin jazz album; and the Cedric Burnside Project's "Descendants of Hill Country" is up for best blues album.

Other crowdfunding outlets have become familiar sights in the Grammy catalog. ArtistShare, a company founded in 2003 that has a partnership with the Blue Note label, is represented in three jazz nominations: the Gil Evans Project's "Lines of Color" and the

Maria Schneider Orchestra's "The Thompson Fields" are up for best large ensemble album, while a saxophone performance by Donny McCaslin on "The Thompson Fields" is a contender for best improvised solo. Three of Ms. Schneider's albums that she made using ArtistShare won Grammys.

Now, to extend Kickstarter's reach in music, the company has hired Molly Neuman, a veteran of the indie scene, as its head of music. In a recent interview at the company's spacious headquarters in a former pencil factory in Greenpoint, Brooklyn, Ms. Neuman described a loose but ambitious mandate to make Kickstarter more useful for listeners seeking new music, and more responsive to the musicians who sign up for it.

"We've established ourselves as a way for creators to get their music kicked off and engage with a community," said Ms. Neuman, who started her career playing drums for the riot grrrl band Bratmobile and was most recently interim president for the American Association of Independent Music, a trade organization for small labels. "When we're thinking about the future, it's really about how we can help artists give fans what they want in a more seamless and helpful way."

One example of how this might work, particularly for onetime stars who retain sizable followings, is a campaign started last week by Naughty by Nature. After campaigns last year by the hip-hop trio De La Soul and the R&B group TLC, two other 1990s giants, Naughty by Nature is looking to raise $100,000 for a 25th-anniversary EP, and offering perks for generous fans, such as being in a music video (for $5,000) or getting a private concert by the group ($10,000).

"Thank God for technology and a loyal fan base," said Vin Rock, a member of Naughty by Nature, whose song "O.P.P." went to No. 6 in 1991. "Because we feel like we don't need to be dependent on a record label anymore."

The group worked closely with Kickstarter in lining up its campaign and reward plans, Ms. Neuman said, and the company wants to make its coaching and promotion expertise available to more musicians, of any size.

For now, however, the most valuable asset that Kickstarter offers to artists may be its position as a conduit for money. Gil Rose, the leader of Boston Modern Orchestra Project and its label, BMOP/sound, which has used Kickstarter for four albums, said that the site is most useful as a supplement to other forms of fund-raising, and functions best when the composers or artists involved activate their own networks online.

Mr. Valentine, of the Nashville Symphony, was more blunt in his assessment of the need for alternative funding types like Kickstarter. "You have to be innovative," he said, "or you die."

Los Angeles Museum Starts a Kickstarter Campaign for a Traveling Egg-Shaped Gallery

BY SOPHIE HAIGNEY | JUNE 9, 2017

IF ALL GOES AS PLANNED — that is, if online backers collectively contribute $75,000 by 12:55 p.m. on July 7 — a tiny egg-shaped museum will be hitched to the back of a truck and make its way from Guatemala City to the Los Angeles County Museum of Art, with stops along the way.

The Los Angeles museum embarked on its first Kickstarter campaign on Wednesday with the goal of funding the unconventional journey of a reproduction of the Nuevo Museo de Arte Contemporáneo, a roughly 8-foot-by-6-foot gallery space in Guatemala City that was once a drive-through kiosk that sold eggs. Since 2012, it has been a center for exhibitions, public programs and community projects — all in a space with a total capacity of four people. The model will be part of the Los Angeles museum's exhibition "A Universal History of Infamy," opening Aug. 20 (though it will likely still be on its journey when the show opens). The exhibition is part of the Getty Foundation-sponsored "Pacific Standard Time: LA/LA," an exploration of Latin American and Latino art by way of Los Angeles.

Artists have used websites like Kickstarter, Indiegogo and GoFundMe to raise money for projects since the inception of digital crowdsourcing. But art institutions, too, are turning to these platforms at a time when many are squeezed for capital.

The Louvre has used such crowdfunding platforms to raise millions of dollars for particular acquisitions. The Queens Museum surpassed a Kickstarter goal on Wednesday for an exhibition titled "Never Built New York." It's a gamble, though. While the Smithsonian raised more than $125,000 for a yoga-themed exhibition at the Freer Gallery of Art and the Arthur M. Sackler Gallery in 2013, it raised only $555 of its goal of $35,000 to bring an Ai Weiwei sculpture to the Smithsonian's Hirshhorn Museum in 2012.

Kickstarter in particular is a risk, because if campaigns don't reach their goal by the appointed deadline they don't keep any of the pledged donations. The Los Angeles County Museum of Art was up for the risk, José Luis Blondet, a curator of the upcoming exhibition, said, because it was aligned with the spirits of Nuevo Museo and the exhibition.

"We thought that a Kickstarter might be a way to generate a sense of belonging," Mr. Blondet said.

Rita Gonzalez, who also organized the exhibition, said the curators had originally planned to bring the reproduced museum the conventional way: in a crate, by air. But the artists who founded Nuevo Museo — Jessica Kairé and Stefan Benchoam — had another idea. Ms. Gonzalez said, "They wanted to turn it into a kind of nomadic museum."

The artists have planned stops in Guatemala, Mexico and Southern California before it will come to rest on a lawn at the Los Angeles museum for six months.

Of course, this roughly 3,000-mile trip will run up a sizable gas bill (not to mention costs for permits, insurance, accommodations, exhibitions and other programming). The museum organizers are betting on internet users — possibly tempted by prizes that include an egg-salad picnic with a curator-led tour and egg-printed tote bags — to raise the funds.

Video Game Raised $148 Million From Fans. Now It's Raising Concerns.

BY LAURA PARKER | MAY 10, 2017

MARK KEARNS, 38, a web designer and gamer from Chicago, stumbled upon a new video game called Star Citizen while online in late 2013. The game, which was in development, promised to revive the spaceflight simulation genre with a sprawling universe for players to explore.

Intrigued, Mr. Kearns decided to pledge money to see the game come to fruition. In total, he donated $175, which gained him access to Star Citizen's alpha version — a playable version of the game in its early stages — plus a virtual ship to use in the game.

Mr. Kearns and others have now vaulted Star Citizen into the record books. Since 2013, the game has quietly amassed more than $148 million in funding — all from regular people who have donated either through the crowdfunding site Kickstarter or through the game's online donations page. The amount is a record for a crowdfunded video game, and one of the largest for any crowdfunded project. Star Citizen's developer, Cloud Imperium Games, has not taken any money from traditional financiers.

"My expectation was that we'd raise around $4 million," said Chris Roberts, 48, the founder of Cloud Imperium Games. "I had investors lined up to help with the rest but Sandy, my wife, told me not to worry about investors — that we'd make it to $20 million. I told her she was crazy, and then it kind of went from there."

Yet the gigantic sum of money has created issues for Star Citizen, which began with a modest goal of raising $500,000 in 2012. As the dollars have mounted, the ambitions of Cloud Imperium Games have grown, and the game's official release has repeatedly been pushed back. Some gamers have demanded refunds. One even filed a formal complaint with the Los Angeles County district attorney's office last year.

NATHANIEL WOOD FOR THE NEW YORK TIMES

Chris Roberts, the founder of Cloud Imperium Games. "I love the idea that people can support a game that wouldn't probably be made by a big studio," he said.

"I'm already building the best game I can," said Mr. Roberts, who acknowledged the bumps. "But imagine — the game I can build with $140 million is going to be very different to the one I could build with $10 million. If I can build a bigger and more robust experience, I will."

Star Citizen's tale highlights the promise and perils of crowdfunded video games, which have become increasingly popular in recent years. Creators have flocked to crowdfunding to make niche games for specific audiences of passionate fans and to interact with gamers earlier in development. Crowdfunding has helped spawn a revival of classic role-playing games like Baldur's Gate and Divinity, which were popular in the late 1990s and early 2000s.

According to Eedar, a video game market research company owned by the NPD Group, about 30,000 successfully funded video game projects were on Kickstarter as of February, and more than $593 million had been pledged to them.

Yet several prominent crowdfunded video games have failed to live up to expectations. Mighty No. 9, a game pitched by the developer Keiji Inafune as a "spiritual successor" to the classic Mega Man action series, raised $4 million, but was delayed several times before being released in 2016 to lukewarm reviews. In 2014, a first-person sword-fighting game called Clang that had raised $500,000 in crowdfunding was canceled when the developer failed to secure additional funding.

"Crowdfunding projects, even those from established developers, are not seen by consumers as a sure bet as they were five years ago," said Patrick Walker, vice president for insights and analytics at Eedar.

Still, for players, giving money to help develop a video game like Star Citizen offers a way into exclusive content — as well as something more emotional.

"Investing in Star Citizen gives you the tantalizing pleasure of looking forward to a deferred enjoyment, a slow, continuous build that stretches out the anticipation and taps into the power of our imagination to fill out the details of its imaginary world," said Frank Lantz, director of the New York University Game Center.

Cloud Imperium Games was founded in 2011 by Mr. Roberts, who has a long history in the video game business. He started making games as a teenager in England, and later gained renown with the Texas-based video game company Origin Systems, where he made the game Wing Commander. Released in 1990, the sci-fi spaceflight simulation game was a critical and commercial success and produced several sequels.

Mr. Roberts later left the games industry to focus on producing film and television projects in Los Angeles. Among other things, he directed the 1999 feature film version of Wing Commander, which starred Freddie Prinze Jr.

After thinking about making Star Citizen for many years, Mr. Roberts was inspired earlier this decade by the success of Minecraft, the hugely popular sandbox game from the Swedish game designer Markus Persson. Mr. Persson first released an alpha version of Minecraft in 2009 for a small sum, then used the proceeds to make adjustments and upgrades. (Mr. Persson sold his video game company Mojang, which makes Minecraft, to Microsoft in 2014 for $2.5 billion.)

"I wanted to do the same thing, without having to deal with a big video game publisher," Mr. Roberts said. "Star Citizen certainly doesn't fit the blockbuster video game mold. I love the idea that people can support a game that wouldn't probably be made by a big studio."

Star Citizen began with a dual crowdfunding effort on its website, plus a Kickstarter campaign in 2012 to increase interest in the project. The Kickstarter campaign ended with just over $2 million raised. From then on, Cloud Imperium Games relied on donations through the Star Citizen site.

The minimum donation to support the game was $5, but players couldn't get a ship to play in the game until they had given at least $30. The highest donation amount was $10,000. Cloud Imperium Games said many people contacted the studio to ask about giving even larger amounts.

By the end of 2013, Star Citizen had raised $35.5 million. At the end of 2015, the amount stood at $104.4 million.

The success of the crowdfunding campaign allowed Mr. Roberts to hire developers worldwide. Cloud Imperium Games has now opened four studios: in Los Angeles; Austin, Tex.; Manchester, England; and Frankfurt. It has hired more than 400 people.

For Matthew Slattery, 18, a Star Citizen backer from South Australia, the idea of being able to play the game while it was still in development was a big draw. He has pledged about $100 to date.

"Getting to learn the process of game development, communicate with the developers and ask questions directly to the best in the field is a very rare opportunity," Mr. Slattery said.

Clifford Zernicek, a 36-year-old designer from Houston, has pledged more than $15,000 to Star Citizen. He said he liked that the development of the game "isn't behind closed doors, like normal publishers."

For now, both donors are willing to wait for Star Citizen — even though its initial release of 2014 was pushed back to 2016, and has been pushed back again. It now has no set release date.

Even so, gamers know Mr. Roberts is adding more features to the game. Mr. Roberts said he was investing in film-level graphics for Star Citizen, as well as building an ever-increasing universe with multiple solar systems and planets for players to explore — all rendered in elaborate detail.

"Of course I have reservations about whether or not Cloud Imperium Games can meet their goals," said Mr. Kearns, the web designer in Chicago. But he added that "after a few updates and patches, I considered my pledge money well spent and anything else that came from the game was a bonus."

Secret Hitler, a Game That Simulates Fascism's Rise, Becomes a Hit

BY JONAH ENGEL BROMWICH | SEPT. 5, 2017

I WAS HOUSE-SITTING for my brother this summer when I saw something suspicious: a box in his living room emblazoned with the words "Secret Hitler."

On his return, I confronted him. "What in God's name is that?" I asked, pointing at the box.

"It's a board game," he said, rolling his eyes.

More specifically, Secret Hitler is a social deduction game, one that has caught on quickly since it began to ship to players last summer. It's like Mafia, or Werewolf, or other games in which players try to identify a traitor in their midst.

In this version, anywhere between five and 10 players are divided into two uneven teams: a larger team of liberals and a smaller team of fascists. (There are no antifa.) One player is chosen as Secret Hitler. The fascists, aware of their leader's identity, work to install him by fooling the liberals, who are kept in the dark.

The makers of the game have raised close to $1.5 million since announcing it on Kickstarter in November 2015. It briefly become the top-selling item in the toy and game category on Amazon when it launched, and it recently sold out its second print run. (The company does not publish sales data, but the money they have raised suggests that they have sold tens of thousands of copies.)

The game was conceived in early 2015 and boosted by its association with Max Temkin, 30, who is one of the creators of the provocative party game Cards Against Humanity. But Secret Hitler benefited from another, unforeseen trend: a significant surge in interest in fascism around the 2016 election, which also saw brisk sales of dystopian literary classics and a rejuvenated discussion of the movement that brought leaders like Hitler and Mussolini to power.

Secret Hitler also arrived amid a renaissance for tabletop games, which have found new purchase among adult consumers. According to Evelyn Rodriguez, a market researcher at Euromonitor International, people 18 and over have been steadily playing more board games in the last several years, with sales continuing to pick up for titles like Settlers of Catan and Enigma.

Independent games in particular have grown in popularity, Euromonitor data showed, as Kickstarter has become a hub for creators with ideas that may be too risky or too strange for traditional publishers. On the crowdfunding platform, creators can raise money while also finding an audience for idiosyncratic titles and getting feedback from potential buyers as games are still in development.

The secret ingredient in Secret Hitler's development was a round of binge-watching. Sometime in late February or early March of 2015, one of its creators, Mike Boxleiter, 32, spent a weekend with the Steven Spielberg-produced World War II mini-series "Band of Brothers."

Mr. Boxleiter, Mr. Temkin and a third creator, Tommy Maranges, had been obsessing over the intricacies of deception games. When Mr. Boxleiter returned to their shared office on Monday after having watched 705 minutes of Americans battling Germans, he had an idea for a new game, based on Hitler's rise to power. The group had a playable prototype of Secret Hitler 48 hours later.

"It was a month before even Hillary announced," Mr. Maranges, 27, said. "It truly was like, what if we made a game about the past, and not about any other time in history."

They set up a Kickstarter campaign on Nov. 23, 2015, with a goal of raising $54,450 to print its first run of the game, with art by Mackenzie Schubert. In 24 hours, it had raised more than twice that amount. By the time the game began shipping, in August 2016, it had attracted more than 30,000 backers, making it one of the five most widely supported tabletop games in Kickstarter's history. (The game is not yet available overseas, but it does not include any Nazi symbols or images of Hitler, making it more likely to be accepted in countries like Germany.)

Though it is easier for edgy games to find support at Kickstarter, even people at the crowdfunding site were unpersuaded by the name at first.

"I advised them not to call it that," said Luke Crane, Kickstarter's head of games. "I said don't call it that. My exact words were perhaps a bit more colorful."

He said that even with the success of the game, he still knew some people who would not play it because of its name. But he added that it was clear that the game's creators had tapped into a topic of discussion in a way that was difficult to achieve, even among the subset that reach to do so.

Secret Hitler's creators are aware that some consumers will not find any humor in the game's title, either because Nazis are not a laughing matter or because of fears about the growing visibility of white supremacists and other extremists since the election of President Trump.

The gamemakers have not been shy about linking the game to the president. At the website, they advise those who "don't think there's anything funny or cool about fascism" to address complaints to the White House. They have also sent copies of the game to senators and released a Trump administration expansion pack, with cards for some members of the administration. It was quickly outpaced by news events, given that there are cards for Stephen K. Bannon and Sean Spicer, who left the White House over the summer.

None of the game's creators, who are based in Chicago, voted for Mr. Trump. Mr. Temkin, who has worked on Democratic campaigns, said he did not think he knew anyone who did — and his victory took the gamemakers by surprise. He said they even felt a twinge of regret about their timing.

"Oh, it's too bad that when this game comes out, Donald Trump won't be relevant to American politics anymore because it would be great marketing for us," Mr. Temkin remembered thinking.

NIRAJ CHOKSHI contributed reporting.

Florence's Answer to Mafia Violence: A Painting's Loving Restoration

BY GAIA PIANIGIANI | MAY 25, 2018

FLORENCE, ITALY — Four years ago, a Florentine restorer happened upon a painting fragment peeking out of an envelope stored in a depository at the city's famed museum, the Uffizi Gallery. It depicted part of a six of spades.

"I used to play cards with my dad and his friends," the restorer, Daniela Lippi, 49, recalled. "That small detail meant something to me right away."

The piece was from "The Card Players" by Bartolomeo Manfredi, an early 17th-century follower of Caravaggio. The painting had been shredded in a 1993 Mafia bombing in the center of Florence that damaged hundreds of art works at the Uffizi. It had been deemed

NADIA SHIRA COHEN FOR THE NEW YORK TIMES

Daniela Lippi putting the final touches on "The Card Players" by Bartolomeo Manfredi at her studio before the painting's re-installment in the Uffizi Gallery in Florence.

unrestorable. The 615 canvas scraps that could be recovered had been set aside.

On Saturday, after months of crowdfunding efforts in Florence, and 10 months of arduous restoration by Ms. Lippi, the painting will be displayed at the Uffizi for the first time since that attack, which killed five residents and wounded dozens, in addition to damaging historic buildings. It is the last of the damaged works to be restored.

When Ms. Lippi opened the envelope she discovered four years ago, the hundreds of painting fragments were still covered with the translucent, Japanese rice paper that custodians had used in 1993 to preserve them.

She realized that at least some of the players' faces could be brought back to life, and decided to undertake a laborious restoration.

Her efforts were aided in 2017, when, with the 25th anniversary of the attack approaching, a local paper began a crowdfunding drive. The publicity campaign used the disfigured face of a player from the painting, and the effort quickly caught on, surpassing its goal and raising 26,000 euros in all.

The city's institutions were also determined to use the campaign to keep the memory of the attack alive and to remind residents that they still needed to fight back against Mafia terrorism.

"For Florence, Italy, and the world, it was such an important event of terror," said Eike Schmidt, the director of the Uffizi. "We can't bring back to life the people left dead, or the heavily damaged paintings. But we can build a memorial for culture against violence and terror."

The Uffizi Gallery gave permission for the restoration, the Scala Archives donated a large photo of the original from which Ms. Lippi could work, and a group of professional restorers helped her.

"It was in such condition that I knew I couldn't bring it back to its original perfection," Ms. Lippi said recently, as she applied the finishing touches to the painting in her Florentine laboratory, magnifying glasses on her eyes and a brush in hand.

NADIA SHIRA COHEN FOR THE NEW YORK TIMES

"I am Florentine, I had seen the Uffizi so many times," said Maurizio Maleci, a fire official who was one of the first on the scene. "But the paintings there no longer existed, the city had been struck at the heart."

For 10 months, mixing digital imagery, modern scanning technology, and old-school color recognition, she learned the painter's most intimate touches by heart.

The 615 fragments amounted to a precious and delicate jigsaw puzzle.

Of them, 500 were cleaned, sewn together and then glued onto a new canvas, forming an imperfect portrait of men dressed in elaborate clothes playing zarro, a betting game popular in the 1500s. The other pieces — too small or damaged to be used — will be preserved.

"The missing pieces are important, to show what happened to it," Ms. Lippi said, referring to the new sand-colored stucco that she has treated to look like a 17th-century canvas. "This painting is the living memory of the attack 25 years ago."

While Ms. Lippi was working, a team of documentary filmmakers recorded her effort. They also launched their own fund-raising drive, called "The Care," to show what it took to care for the painting.

"This is not just a restored painting," Luca Galassi, one of the documentary makers, said. "It's a symbol of strength and rebirth of a community still years on."

For the coming week, the Uffizi will host an immersive installation that will allow visitors to relive that night — May 27, 1993 — when a blast close to the museum reverberated through the narrow medieval streets and arches. A quarter of the Uffizi's art works suffered damage. Paintings were cut by flying glass, ancient statues were mutilated, and vast cracks opened in the museum walls overlooking the street where a Sicilian mobster had detonated a Fiat van loaded with more than 600 pounds of explosives at 1 a.m. on a Wednesday.

Decades later, judges established that the attack was part of a strategy by the Sicilian Mafia to hit landmarks in retaliation for the government's imposition of strict rules, including isolation, against jailed Mafiosi.

Most Florentines clearly remember that night. Some recall the detonation, which could be heard from miles away, and others the potent shock wave it caused. The explosion left a deep crater where the Fiat had been parked, hidden from view near the gallery. The detonation was so violent the asphalt was pulverized into rocks and sand; a piece of the van was found across the river.

Rescuers recall hundreds of dumbfounded residents coming out on the streets. It took hours before Florentines realized that it was a car bomb. The early-morning news still spoke of a possible gas tank explosion.

It was around 6 a.m. that day that firefighters walked into the Uffizi Gallery with the museum's curators, recalled Maurizio Maleci, a fire official who filmed the aftermath.

There was total darkness. The outer gate looked intact, he recalled, but as they walked deeper into the corridors, they could hear the sound of broken glass crunching underfoot.

"I am Florentine, I had seen the Uffizi so many times," Mr. Maleci said. "But the paintings there no longer existed, the city had been struck at the heart."

"The Card Players" was scattered in tiny fragments around the floor, he said. A nearby canvas was torn apart.

In a neoclassical room, portions of the stucco fell from the ornate barrel-vaulted roof and an ancient Greek sculpture had its legs cut off from the window glass and wooden frame.

"The devastation was such that I thought we had lost them," Mr. Maleci said. His voice cracking, he remembered the small kindnesses of Florentines, who offered firefighters coffee as they labored over the rubble.

And in the following weeks, Florence fought back. The museum personnel searched the floors on their knees, separating the plaster and bricks from pieces of canvas and marble, and gently collected them in wooden trays.

The paintings that sustained the heaviest damage were from the Caravaggio school, whose iconic colors were dark. Determining which fragment belonged to which painting proved to be an enormous task, officials remembered.

Parts of the Uffizi reopened just 20 days later, but while it was shut other museums opened extra hours to offer visitors the city's best face.

"Younger generations don't know much about those bloody years," said Mr. Schmidt, the Uffizi director. "This is also for them to know that the mafia still exists, and it's a risk we need to reckon with."

In Brazil, 'Queer Museum' Is Censored, Debated, Then Celebrated

BY ERNESTO LONDOÑO | AUG. 26, 2018

RIO DE JANEIRO — Had it gone as planned, an exhibition that opened last year in Brazil — which included a drawing of smiling children with the words "transvestite" and "gay child" stenciled across them — would likely have been a mere blip in the country's lively art scene.

Gaudêncio Fidélis, the curator who assembled the 264 pieces that made up the "Queer Museum" exhibition, had expected at least a whiff of criticism for the art show. But nothing could have prepared him for the torrent of controversy that set off protests and shut down the exhibition within days.

Even after the show was closed, the storm of criticism kept the

DADO GALDIERI FOR THE NEW YORK TIMES

Lining up in Rio de Janeiro to see the "Queer Museum" exhibition.

project in the news, inciting a heated, monthslong national debate about freedom of expression and what qualifies as art.

After nearly a year of arguments, the exhibition — which also included a painting of the Virgin Mary cradling a monkey, and sacramental wafers with words like "vagina" and "penis" written on them in neat cursive — reopened this month in Parque Lage, a public park in Rio de Janeiro that is also home to a renowned art school.

As he stepped to the podium earlier this month to preside over the opening ceremony, Mr. Fidélis looked ebullient as he flashed a victory sign.

"In the face of censorship and the shutdown of 'Queer Museum,' there was no alternative but to react and believe the future had this victory in store for us," he said before a jubilant crowd, awash in the colors of the gay pride flag.

Despite his claim of an outright win, the opposition has no intention of surrendering the fight. Even as he spoke, a small group of protesters heckled him from a few feet away. They held Brazilian flags and religious signs, including one showing a smiling, white couple with three children under the words: "God created man in his image; he created a man and a woman."

The contentious exhibition has cast a spotlight on the battle over gay and transgender rights in Brazil, Latin America's largest nation.

Over the past decade, the region has marked notable gains for the movement for legal equality for gay and transgender people. Brazil, which began recognizing same-sex unions in 2004, became in 2013 one of the first countries in the Americas to legalize same-sex marriage.

São Paulo, the country's largest city, hosts the world's largest gay pride parade, and Rio de Janeiro has long been a popular destination for gay tourists.

But in Brazil, gay and transgender advocates have made inroads mainly through litigation, rather than legislation, while voters have elected increasingly conservative politicians.

There is one openly gay lawmaker in Brazil's Congress, while 199

DADO GALDIERI FOR THE NEW YORK TIMES

Protesters were among the first to arrive on the exhibition's official opening day. They chanted "blasphemy cannot hide in art."

of the 513 representatives in the lower House belong to the so-called Evangelical caucus, which includes members who have championed conversion therapy for gays.

"The correlation between legal changes and greater social acceptance of L.G.B.T.I. people is not straightforward," said Fabrice Houdart, a human rights officer at the United Nations who focuses on sexual orientation and gender identity issues like intersexuality. "In several places in Latin America, legal rights have changed much more quickly than attitudes."

As the political arena has become increasingly hostile to the gay rights movement, activists have turned to the arts and the private sector to build grass-roots support.

That was one of the motivating factors that drove Fabio Szwarcwald, the head of Parque Lage art school, to resurrect the "Queer Museum" exhibition.

The school has never shied away from controversy. Founded in the 1970s while Brazil was under military rule, it became a hub for artists and intellectuals who pushed the boundaries of criticism during an era in which the press and speech were heavily censored.

To fund the show, Mr. Szwarcwald started a crowdfunding campaign, which raised more than $327,000, a record in Brazil.

The first fight over the "Queer Museum" exhibition erupted just days after it opened in early September last year at the cultural center of Banco Santander, one of the largest banks in Brazil, in Porto Alegre, a city in southern Brazil.

Many of the protesters were from the Free Brazil Movement, a conservative group that played a leading role in calling for the impeachment of leftist president Dilma Rousseff in 2016. They denounced artwork they saw as demeaning Catholic symbols and promoting zoophilia and pedophilia.

The church took up the cause, too.

The archdiocese of Porto Alegre issued a statement calling the works an "attack on the Judeo-Christian culture that contributed to the cultural formation of the West." It added: "In times of terrorism and intolerance, you do not build bridges with aggression and disrespect for what is most intimate and sacred in the other: their faith and their body."

As dueling camps of protesters gathered outside the cultural center last year, and the bank's inboxes were flooded with critical messages, executives at Banco Santander decided to pull the plug on the show.

"We offer sincere apologies to those who saw disrespect for faith and symbols in the exhibit 'Queer Museum,' " the bank said in a statement to its customers. "This is not part of our worldview or the values we support."

Federal prosecutors took the bank to task for shutting down the exhibition and called on it to reopen it at once.

"Freedom of expression constitutes a constitutionally guaranteed right that is vital to human dignity," prosecutors wrote in an opinion.

But prosecutors could not compel the bank to act, and the opinion was disregarded.

If the bank had enjoyed the final word, Mr. Fidélis said, it would have set a dangerous precedent for freedom of expression in Brazil at a moment when its democracy is under strain amid deep political polarization. He argued that it would have also sent a chilling message to gay and transgender Brazilians, who are often the victims of hate crimes.

Mr. Fidélis first tried to move the exhibition to the Rio Art Museum. But soon after Mr. Fidélis began negotiating with museum officials, Marcelo Crivella, the mayor of Rio de Janeiro and an evangelical preacher, said the institution, which receives public funding, would not host it.

That is when the art school stepped in.

At an evening preview of the exhibition inside its new home in Rio de Janeiro, Bianca Kalutor, 30, a transgender woman, beamed with pride.

The provocative, transgressive pieces surrounding her made her feel at home — and safe, she said, giving her a sense of belonging that has eluded her from childhood.

"There are all these spaces in which queer people are questioned," she said. "Being trans, you develop an ability to enter and leave spaces without being noticed."

The following morning, on the day of the exhibition's formal opening, a couple dozen protesters were among the first to arrive at Parque Lage. Carrying signs that said "zoophilia" and "pedophilia," they chanted: "blasphemy cannot hide in art."

Their chants were soon drowned out by a collective of female drummers.

Anticipating the possibility of violence, Parque Lage had hired additional security personnel and had an ambulance on standby. David Miranda, the city's sole openly gay council member, took the opportunity to hand out campaign fliers seeking support for his bid for a seat in Congress.

"The L.G.B.T. population is starting to awaken politically," Mr.

DADO GALDIERI FOR THE NEW YORK TIMES

The exhibition incited a national debate about freedom of expression, about what qualifies as art and about gay and transgender rights.

Miranda said. "We need people to take notice of the violence that is happening on a daily basis."

By the time the speeches were over, shortly after noon, the line to enter the exhibition stretched for well over a block. During its inaugural weekend, "Queer Museum," which will be on display until Sept. 16, drew nearly 7,000 visitors.

"This turnout is evidence that Cariocas are not going to accept censorship," Mr. Szwarcwald said, using the term for Rio de Janeiro residents.

But there was one final obstacle that troubled Mr. Szwarcwald, a father of two young boys. At the request of an evangelical City Council member, a judge had issued an order the day before the opening banning children 14 and under from visiting the exhibit.

On Tuesday, after another judge suspended that order, Mr. Szwarcwald and Mr. Fidélis smiled as they tore up the sign noting the prohibition.

CHAPTER 3

Crowdfunding for Change: Activism and Philanthropy

Crowdfunding has been successful for philanthropic endeavors and political activism alike. The social aspect of crowdfunding, and its capacity to raise awareness of a cause in addition to funds, has benefited these campaigns in particular. The accessibility of community-sourced fund-raising also empowers those who feel unsure of how to help: They are able to give financial support to aid programs for distant natural disasters or families separated at border crossings.

A Crowdfunding Campaign Tries to Save Greece

BY KATIE ROGERS | JUNE 30, 2015

GREECE WAS ON the edge of a deadline to pay 1.5 billion euros (about $1.75 billion) back to the International Monetary Fund, and a crowd-funding campaign called Greek Bailout Fund wanted to help.

The campaign, set up on the fund-raising website Indiegogo, had raised more than €487,000 by early Wednesday — not an insignificant amount of money, but also not even 1 percent of the campaign's goal, with six days to go.

The campaign was started by an Indiegogo user named Thom

Feeney, who identifies himself as a 29-year-old working in a shoe shop in Britain.

"Let's just get Greece sorted," Mr. Feeney wrote on the campaign page. "All this dithering over Greece is getting boring."

Crowdfunding, or raising money online from many individuals who each give small amounts, has financed a number of high-profile projects in recent years. Some campaigns seem to be intentionally wacky — like the one in 2011 that raised $67,000 to pay for a RoboCop statue in Detroit — while others seek to make the world a better place.

But a crowdfunding campaign to bail out a country seems to be a first, according to Anindya Ghose, a professor of information technology and marketing at New York University's Stern School of Business, who has been researching crowdfunding for the past six years.

"It's very unique," Mr. Ghose wrote in an email.

In at least one way, though, the campaign and the reaction to the crisis in Greece fit into what Mr. Ghose has seen in his research: Altruism is a key motivating factor inspiring people to donate.

"It's hard to put a price on that kind of support," Mr. Ghose said. "It's priceless."

Gifts of different sizes to the Indiegogo fund yield different rewards for the donor. A €10 donation gets a bottle of ouzo, while a donation of a million euros buys "a lot of gratitude from the citizens of Europe."

Supporters are using the hashtag #crowdfundgreece to spread the word on Twitter.

One poster, @edrex, said: "Crowdfund the Greek bailout. If it fails, you get your money back. If it works, you're a part of history. No-brainer"

Some pondered whether the campaign would raise the €1.5 billion. "Every time I refresh the page, the numbers are up. Is this going to work?" @LisaFreiburg posted.

The expert opinion: Absolutely not. And even if it did, the €1.5 billion that was due Tuesday is a tiny fraction of Greece's total debt, which Reuters estimated at €242.8 billion. Another payment, €3.5 billion to the European Central Bank, is due in July.

"Unfortunately, it does not have much teeth," Mr. Ghose said. "Even if it goes viral, there is just no way this campaign can lead to a meaningful amount that will truly bail out the government."

No harm in trying, though.

Obama Turns to Crowdfunding to Aid Fleeing Syrians

BY MICHAEL D. SHEAR | OCT. 6, 2015

WASHINGTON — As Syrian refugees continue to flee the violence at home, President Obama is turning to the modern tools of Silicon Valley entrepreneurship as a supplement to the more traditional means of humanitarian relief.

At the request of officials from the White House Office of Digital Strategy, the crowdfunding website Kickstarter has begun its first social service campaign aimed at raising money for the United Nations refugee agency on behalf of Syrian refugees.

Visitors to the site, which is better known for helping inventors and filmmakers, can contribute $15 to buy a sleeping bag, $70 for an emergency rescue kit, or $160, which the site says could pay for a refugee's shelter in a "well-built group tent, complete with sleeping bag and mat."

The weeklong campaign, which began Tuesday, had raised more than $550,000 as of that night for a nonprofit organization that supports the United Nations refugee agency, an amount the site said had already helped more than 2,000 people.

In a blog post on the White House website, Joshua Miller, an official in the digital strategy office, wrote that the Kickstarter effort — along with a similar one with Instacart, an online grocery delivery service — is an effort to follow up on Mr. Obama's plea for Americans to do their part on behalf of the refugees.

White House officials said the online fund-raising would not replace the government's efforts or other programs to help manage the refugee crisis. The administration has said it plans to increase by 10,000 the number of Syrian refugees admitted into the United States in the next year and to further expand the number of refugees admitted from other countries.

The administration has said it will also continue to contribute money to help confront the crisis overseas. Officials said the United States was the largest single donor of humanitarian assistance, having given about $4.5 billion to support those escaping the violence.

The refugee agency's appeals for money for the Syria crisis have raised less than half what is needed. Appeals for other refugee crises, including those in Darfur and Central African Republic, which receive far less media attention and are not part of the Kickstarter campaign, face a worse predicament.

White House officials noted that in 1885, hundreds of thousands of Americans donated small sums to pay for a $2.5 million base for the Statue of Liberty. "Just like we banded together in 1885, we can join together to provide shelter, food and medical assistance to these people in need," Mr. Miller wrote in his blog post. "It's the American thing to do."

SOMINI SENGUPTA contributed reporting from New York.

Crowdfunding Helps Rescue Refugees Upended by Travel Ban

BY NICHOLAS KULISH AND NATHANIEL POPPER | FEB. 9, 2017

TRAPPED IN AN AIRPORT terminal in Jordan by President Trump's travel ban, Hanan Isweiri fretted that as a Libyan citizen she would not be able to return to her husband and three children in Colorado. She wondered if she could complete the doctorate she had worked toward for seven years. Most of all, she feared for her 1-year-old son, who was having an allergic reaction but was not permitted to leave the airport.

Just about the only thing she did not have to worry about — despite staying in airport hotels in Jordan and Turkey, and repeatedly booking and rebooking intercontinental flights in those chaotic early days — was money. Friends had set up a GoFundMe web page, raising

SUSAN STAVA FOR THE NEW YORK TIMES

Demonstrators at a march against President Trump's travel ban in Manhattan last month. In dozens of cases, immigrants and residents affected by the ban have gotten financial assistance from friends and neighbors through crowdfunding sites.

$5,366 to help defray the significant costs she incurred as a result of the ban.

"Some friends do a fund-raising site for me, and I believe without this I would never make it," said Ms. Isweiri, 41, who made it back to Colorado on Sunday, two days after a federal judge put a halt, for now, on the travel ban.

After Mr. Trump's executive order, individual lawyers volunteered their time and expertise at airports around the country. Large organizations like the American Civil Liberties Union, which had seen a boom in fund-raising after Mr. Trump's election victory, have helped mount legal challenges.

But the financial dislocation for ordinary people like Ms. Isweiri, a Ph.D. student at Colorado State University who was in Libya for her father's funeral when Mr. Trump signed off on the ban, was enormous. In dozens of cases, crowdfunding sites allowed friends, neighbors and complete strangers to fill the gap and cover the expenses that otherwise might have unwound the financial security of immigrants and residents affected by the ban.

Because of the decentralized nature of the campaigns, it is hard to say exactly how many have started since the change in immigration policy. But the largest crowdfunding site, GoFundMe, and a company it recently acquired, CrowdRise, have seen more than 50 new campaigns that have raised nearly $1.5 million related to the executive order, which halted travel from seven predominantly Muslim countries for 90 days and barred Syrian refugees indefinitely. An appeals court in San Francisco is reviewing the order.

YouCaring, a smaller GoFundMe competitor, is also hosting several campaigns, including one that has raised nearly $7,000 for a Syrian woman who had been approved to resettle in Little Rock, Ark. A British site, CrowdJustice, sped up its opening in the United States after Mr. Trump's executive order. The first American campaign on the site raised $36,000 to pay for the lawyers of two Yemeni brothers who were deported after arriving at Dulles International Airport in Virginia.

In just the last few years, crowdfunding has increasingly become a regular part of the public response to humanitarian crises like floods, mass shootings or, in this case, the fallout from a presidential order.

GoFundMe has, on its own, helped attract more than $3.4 billion in donations from 30 million donors since it was founded in 2010 — more than what has been pledged on well-known crowdfunding sites like Kickstarter, which focus more on helping entrepreneurs and artists.

"We are the social safety net for everyone who falls through the cracks," said Rob Solomon, the chief executive of GoFundMe, which is based in Redwood City, just south of San Francisco. "No matter how great the NGOs and government agencies are, a lot of people will fall through the cracks."

GoFundMe takes 5 percent of the funds raised for administrative fees and an additional 2.9 percent for credit card processing. It defends the fees by pointing to the costs involved in maintaining the site, and building systems for vetting potential fund-raising campaigns. YouCaring charges 3 percent for credit card processing.

These campaigns have been dogged by questions about whether they represent the most efficient way to get money to people in need of help. Existing charities have complained that crowdfunding has siphoned money to the saddest personal stories, as opposed to the established institutions that provide broad support after emergencies. The sites have also faced criticism over their level of oversight to ensure that money ends up where it is supposed to go.

Ethan Mollick, a professor at the Wharton School at the University of Pennsylvania who has studied crowdfunding, said the individual nature of the campaigns could lower the level of accountability around spending.

When Eric Martinez and Jen Thorson, the founders of the company Modjoul, realized that their employee Nazanin Zinouri, a recent Ph.D. graduate of Clemson University, was trapped in her native Iran, they set up a GoFundMe page with a $30,000 goal to help get her back, and were met with criticism over what some users of the site perceived as a very high figure.

"You've already raised $12,000 in 2 mere days, what is that for?" a user, under the name Kimba Essence, asked in a post last week. "Where is the disclosure on what you are doing with $12,000?"

Mr. Martinez said that people were underestimating the costs — not just for all the international cellphone calls, printing bills for legal filings and the $3,200 for same-day flights from Tehran to Frankfurt to Boston, but also for an immigration lawyer to work on her case in what was expected to be a protracted legal battle. Also anticipated: months of car and rent payments while she waited without a job to get back into the country. (She made it back this past Sunday.)

"Everybody said too much money, so we lowered it" to $15,000, Mr. Martinez said. "The only negative about it is the trolls come on," he added. "The uneducated, espousing their views, not knowing what it takes."

But trolls can also spur fund-raising. After someone on Twitter told the actor and former White House employee Kal Penn, "You don't belong in this country," he went on CrowdRise and asked for $2,500 for the International Rescue Committee. He ended up raising over $800,000.

Lawyers in Dallas, who set up a "war room" at the local airport to help detained travelers, raised $34,000 to pay for the expenses associated with the operation. Another $25,000 was raised for a Yemeni girl separated from her family.

Mr. Mollick said the sites had been a promising new venue for fund-raising because they allow for a wider array of innovative approaches to emergencies, in ways that offer donors a more personal sense of investment.

"The crowd tends to select a greater variety of things, things that can be really good or really bad," he said. "With expert money, you tend to get the same result every time."

Taking Guns Off the Streets, $100 at a Time

BY CLAIRE MARTIN | JULY 7, 2017

JAMES RONALD LEE III pulled his cherry red Volkswagen up to a pair of detectives from the Los Angeles Police Department in a parking lot in South Los Angeles. The detectives pulled a handgun, a rifle and a sock stuffed with ammunition from the trunk.

Mr. Lee had kept the guns in a liquor store he once owned and did not have a use for them anymore. "I don't want them around my house, because anything could happen," he said. Mr. Lee received a $100 Target gift card for each weapon.

He was part of a one-day gun buyback organized by Mayor Eric Garcetti's Office of Gang Reduction and Youth Development. That day in May, the police collected 772 guns in a program financed in part by a nonprofit called Gun by Gun that uses crowdfunding to help take guns off the streets.

Gun by Gun is the brainchild of Ian Johnstone, a tech entrepreneur, and Eric King, an expert on innovation. The two friends use contemporary technology and financing to address the vexing problem of gun violence. Since its founding in 2013, Gun by Gun donors have given a total of $100,000 toward the purchase and destruction of 1,100 weapons.

The goal of gun buybacks, which gained popularity in the 1990s, is to coax people to turn over the most lethal types of weapons. A 2012 Congressional Research Service report put the number of guns in the country at 310 million.

Given the scale of the problem, Mr. Johnstone and Mr. King, both 35, acknowledge that buybacks are not a definitive solution, but they see any reduction in the rate of gun ownership in a community as a boon. "Every $100 donated means one less gun on the streets," Mr. Johnstone said.

For him, the issue of gun violence couldn't be more personal. In 1992, when he was 10 and living on Staten Island, his father was shot in the back in a botched robbery while on a business trip in San Francisco. He died from his injuries a month later.

Mr. Johnstone's mother, Katina Johnstone, founded New Yorkers Against Gun Violence, a legislative advocacy group. She also helped organize the first Silent March in 1994, during which nearly 40,000 pairs of shoes were placed at the United States Capitol — one for every victim of gun violence the previous year. Mr. Johnstone's father's shoes were among them.

Leading up to the march, the family's basement was filled with shoes, Mr. Johnstone recalled. As a child, he accompanied his mother on trips to Albany to talk to state representatives. She made an unsuccessful bid for Congress in 2000, running as a Democrat on Staten Island.

Mr. Johnstone said he became frustrated with advocacy as a solution to gun violence. "I came to see it tends to go nowhere," he said. In his view, there has not been major federal legislation on the issue since the 1994 assault weapons ban, which expired in 2004.

He and Mr. King, who met as students at Binghamton University, began to mull over other approaches to gun violence in 2013. Mr. Johnstone was at the time the chief operating officer of the start-up he founded, Blissmo, which delivers organic and healthful products to consumers; Mr. King was doing postdoctoral work in physics at the University of California, Berkeley.

Mr. Johnstone now works for TruBrain, which makes drinks and bars meant to enhance cognitive function. Mr. King worked at the United States Agency for International Development until last year, and is now in the private sector.

"What are the techie solves we could come up with for this?" is how Mr. King describes their mind-set. The answer: a Kickstarter campaign for gun buybacks.

Gun by Gun, they decided, would be "about getting guns off the street, but also about creating community and giving people a sense of agency," Mr. Johnstone said.

They helped raise money for a gun buyback program in San Francisco, which got them started, and have done so in other cities, including Los Angeles.

The duo looked at what the social entrepreneurship organizations Watsi, Kiva and DonorsChoose were doing and discovered that crowdfunding was not as easy as it looked.

"People tend to think you publish a page and then the internet just sends people there and the money starts rolling in," Mr. Johnstone said. "The reality is that it takes a lot of old-school organizing," like reaching out and asking people for donations directly. He said one of the unwritten rules of crowdfunding is that success hinges on a campaign raising 20 to 40 percent of its goal within the first 48 hours.

"You need to kind of manufacture that, find the people who are going to support it early on and get commitments so that you can launch with momentum," he said.

The Gun by Gun founders said they encountered limitations with crowdfunding platforms such as Indiegogo and Tilt, which is now defunct. They wanted the ability, for instance, to add off-line donations into a campaign's coffers.

They turned to NationBuilder, a software networking company geared toward political campaigns, through which they designed a custom platform.

Mr. Johnstone and Mr. King have struggled against the perception that gun buybacks are ineffective. For years, buybacks attracted older gun owners turning over defunct weapons, not the people or guns typically involved in crimes, said Dr. Garen Wintemute, director of the violence prevention research program and a professor of medicine at the University of California, Davis. Also, there were stories of people selling their guns and using the money to buy better ones.

Buybacks have become more effective, Dr. Wintemute said, as organizers have offered bigger financial incentives for newer, higher-powered weapons. At the Los Angeles buyback, for instance, those surrendering assault weapons received $200 gift cards, twice the amount for revolvers and other handguns. An Uzi submachine gun and an anti-tank rocket launcher were among the weapons turned in.

Cities are using buybacks as part of broad crime-reduction strategies. In an interview, Mr. Garcetti said he saw buybacks as a way to send a positive message.

"It gives us an opportunity to state our cultural values, that we believe guns should not just be lying around unprotected, unwanted," he said. "That we can try to make a dent in the number of guns on the streets of L.A."

Gun by Gun, he said, adds financial strength that previous buybacks have not had. "A lot of times we've run out of gift cards," Mr. Garcetti said of past buybacks. Money raised by Gun by Gun in May allowed his office to purchase an additional 100 guns, he said.

Mr. Johnstone compares crowdfunded gun buybacks to volunteering for beach cleanups and at soup kitchens. "Is the beach cleanup going to make a dent in climate change?" Mr. Johnstone said. "Probably not. But it's an opportunity for like-minded people to get together and on a very small scale, make a difference."

Similarly, there's a limit to what crowdfunded buybacks can accomplish. They "won't end gun violence," he said. "But they can help reduce the likelihood of it in any given community, and they help people feel engaged."

Women Ask 'What if It Were Me?' and Rush to Aid Separated Families

BY ANNIE CORREAL | JULY 20, 2018

JULIE SCHWIETERT COLLAZO unrolled a giant sheet of paper at her kitchen table in Long Island City, Queens, on a recent morning. As her three children played nearby, she began going down a list of names written on it in purple marker.

"Hillary Estefany. Hillary Alejandra," she read, explaining they were 19-year-old twins whose brother was separated from them after they illegally crossed the Southwest border. Both were being held in Eloy, Ariz., on $15,000 bonds. "Delmi. She's from Guatemala," she went on. "Separation case. $30,000."

Just over three weeks ago, Ms. Schwietert Collazo launched a crowdfunding campaign on behalf of another woman detained in

GABRIELLA ANGOTTI-JONES/THE NEW YORK TIMES

Julie Schwietert Collazo, right, initially began a campaign to get Yeni González out of immigration detention, but her efforts have expanded.

Eloy, Yeni González, a Guatemalan migrant whose children had been taken from her at the border as part of the Trump Administration's zero tolerance policy. Ms. Schwietert Collazo was spurred into action after she heard Ms. González's lawyer on the radio. While Ms. González was being held in Arizona on a $7,500 bond, her three children were living in a foster home in New York.

"The subtext was if we could get her here, she could get her kids back," Ms. Schwietert Collazo said.

She set about getting Ms. González to New York. She asked a few mothers she had just met at a donation drive for separated children — and then the public — to help post Ms. González's $7,500 bond. Yeni González was the first woman to have her bond paid by the New York women.

Like the Texas-based nonprofit Refugee and Immigrant Center for Education and Legal Services, or RAICES, which raised more than $20 million after launching a Facebook fund-raiser to cover one detained parent's $1,500 bond, the New York group soon exceeded its once modest goal. As of this week, Ms. Schwietert Collazo's group, which has gone from being called the Yeni González Support Team, to Immigrant Families Together, has raised more than $300,000. They call themselves "a network of Americans committed to rapid response unification of families separated by the 'zero tolerance' policy."

Sara Farrington, a playwright, joined the group and "blitzed mom groups within 100 miles of here" on Facebook to raise money. "People ask me, 'Why this?' 'Why aren't you focusing on the midterms?' I think it comes back to empathy," she said. "To the gut punch of a mom separated from her 5-year-old. The reason that this has exploded, I truly think, is that moms have put themselves in that situation. It has hit a primitive motherly nerve. I think it all stems from, 'What if it were me?' "

Ms. Schwietert Collazo, a former social worker, is now a writer and editor. She launched the Yeni González crowdfunding campaign on June 25. Days later, she paid her bond, and Ms. González was released to her lawyer, José Orochena, in Eloy, and set out for New York.

MARIAN CARRASQUERO/THE NEW YORK TIMES

Meghan Finn is co-artistic director of the Tank, a nonprofit theater in Midtown, and she is now juggling running rehearsals with taking calls about detained immigrant women and their families.

Other women in the Eloy Detention Center learned of Mr. Orochena through Ms. González, who gave them her lawyer's contact information before she was released. Someone typed it up at a library in the detention center, printed 50 copies, and circulated them, Mr. Orochena said.

As the lawyer was flooded with calls, he passed along women's names to Ms. Schwietert Collazo and her group. And so began their round-the-clock work to release and reunite the mothers of Eloy with their children. For each woman they learned about, the organizers launched a crowdfunding campaign in her name.

To date, the group has raised funds through a mix of crowdfunding and private donors — to cover the bonds of 12 women. It has also arranged for them to be driven by volunteers to wherever their children were sent, even if it was thousands of miles from Eloy. Most cannot fly because immigration authorities have held onto their photo identification.

The group has also provided the newly reunited families with housing and pro bono attorneys in the states where they have ended up, Ms. Schwietert Collazo said, creating, in the process, a broad network of helpers. "With the rabbis in Tennessee," she said into her phone at one point this week, "we should be set."

But now, the group's role may be changing. The federal government is hastily putting families back together in order to meet a court-ordered deadline to reunite all separated families by July 26. And the group in New York is getting calls for new kinds of help from all over the country.

This week, a lawyer made an urgent request for medical care for two girls, 2 and 6, who were on the road to Maryland after being reunited with a parent, but had been running high fevers. Another lawyer needed diapers and wipes.

Meghan Finn, the group member in charge of coordinating the women's travel after they are released from Eloy, said what they had been hearing was distressing.

After being transported over long distances to be reunited, often without much food or sleep, many families had been released in government offices, airports and bus stations, with their ankle monitors and a handful of paperwork from Immigration and Customs Enforcement, and little more than the clothes in which they crossed the border.

"They're getting dropped off at Greyhound stations at random times," said Ms. Finn, co-artistic director of the Tank, a nonprofit theater in Midtown Manhattan.

"Listen, this is our job. This is our job because our government did something really heinous to these families, and it's not just about putting them on a bus."

Other than Ms. Schwietert Collazo's husband, Francisco Collazo — a refugee from Cuba who arrived on the Mariel boatlift — the group members are all women, most of them mothers. As their days have been consumed with helping separated families, their partners and parents have taken over child care duties, cooking meals, giving the children haircuts.

“My mom refers to the kitchen as the ‘immigration office,’ ” said Ms. Finn, who lives in Kensington, Brooklyn, with her husband and their two young sons.

Ms. Schwietert Collazo remembers checking with her husband before she launched the first campaign. “I said, ‘We both have to be all in on this. Because it’s something that’s going to take over our lives.’ But I don’t think either of us expected it would be to this extent.”

Meeting the women they have bonded out has revealed the toll of separation and detention, Ms. Finn said. “They’re losing their hair. Their hands are peeling. They’re malnourished. It takes them a while to eat properly.”

So the group has continued raising funds to get more mothers out of Eloy, even as the immigration authorities there have kept increasing the bonds. Delmi’s bond, $30,000, is about four times as much as Ms. González’s bond. “It’s the highest one I’ve seen,” Ms. Schwietert Collazo said.

On Tuesday, Ms. Finn sat with her laptop in a narrow dressing room at Tank on West 36th Street — that day’s immigration office. As actors rehearsed to music onstage, she got a text message from Ms. Schwietert Collazo. Two more bonds had been posted, including one that would have expired the next day.

“Yes! Yes!” Ms. Finn said, slapping the counter. “Beautiful. We’re going to get these ladies out!”

She picked up the phone and called a group member on the West Coast to start organizing the women’s travel.

The next day, Delmi’s bond was covered, too — all $30,000 of it. The actress Kristen Bell closed the gap, with a $4,207 donation.

GoFundMe Campaign for Christine Blasey Ford Takes Off After Testimony

BY MAGGIE ASTOR | SEPT. 27, 2018

A GOFUNDME CAMPAIGN set up on behalf of Christine Blasey Ford drew more than $200,000 in donations in the hours immediately after she mentioned it during her testimony to the Senate Judiciary Committee on Thursday, more money than it had gained in the past eight days.

As of 5 p.m., the campaign "Help Christine Blasey Ford," one of at least two set up on her behalf, had raised more than $378,000 total — up from $175,000 when the hearing began at 10 a.m., according to a spokeswoman for the crowdfunding website.

The GoFundMe campaigns came up after Rachel Mitchell, a prosecutor who questioned Dr. Blasey on behalf of Republican members of the committee, asked who had paid for a polygraph examination Dr. Blasey took as part of her sexual assault accusation against Judge Brett M. Kavanaugh, President Trump's Supreme Court nominee.

"I'm aware that there's been several GoFundMe sites," Dr. Blasey told Ms. Mitchell in response, adding that the money would be used for her family's expenses as a result of her speaking out, including security protection, but that she did not yet know how to access or retrieve it.

Dr. Blasey and her family, facing death threats, have moved out of their home and hired a security detail since she went public with her allegation against Judge Kavanaugh.

Dr. Blasey's lawyers, Michael R. Bromwich and Debra Katz, interjected to say that her legal team had paid for the polygraph — "as is routine," Mr. Bromwich said — and that they were both working pro bono.

"We are not being paid," he said, "and we have no expectations of being paid."

A spokeswoman for GoFundMe, Katherine Cichy, said the company had verified the authenticity of the "Help Christine Blasey Ford"

ERIN SCHAFF FOR THE NEW YORK TIMES

Christine Blasey Ford during the Senate Judiciary Committee hearing on Thursday.

campaign and one other, which ran from Sept. 18 to Sept. 20 and raised $209,987 explicitly for her security costs. It was shut down after it exceeded its $175,000 goal.

"We are working directly with all campaign organizers and guarantee the funds raised will be transferred directly to the Ford family," she said. (Dr. Blasey is sometimes referred to by her married name, Ford.)

Ms. Cichy said Dr. Blasey's family had been designated as the beneficiary of both campaigns, and that the funds could not be withdrawn by or redirected to anyone else. The organizers, with GoFundMe's help, will coordinate with Dr. Blasey's family to transfer the funds, she said.

Muslim Groups Raise Thousands for Pittsburgh Synagogue Shooting Victims

BY MATTHEW HAAG | OCT. 29, 2018

TWO MUSLIM ORGANIZATIONS have raised nearly $200,000 to help victims and their families following the shooting massacre at the Tree of Life Synagogue in Pittsburgh on Saturday.

The online fund-raiser was part of a broad outpouring of assistance in response to the anti-Semitic attack, which killed 11 people and left six others injured, including blood drives, vigils and a separate crowdfunding campaign that has raised hundreds of thousands of dollars.

Tarek El-Messidi, a Chicago-based activist, said he learned of the synagogue shooting in a call Saturday morning from a friend who runs the Muslim fund-raising website LaunchGood. His friend asked Mr. El-Messidi if he could do something to help the victims, and he agreed.

Within two hours, he had created an online campaign with the backing of two Muslim groups, CelebrateMercy, where he is the founding director, and MPower Change. He set an initial goal of $25,000, which was promptly shattered as donations flooded in.

Mr. El-Messidi said he was able to jump-start the campaign and bring in donations so quickly because he has unfortunately done this before. He created a LaunchGood fund-raiser last year that collected $136,000 to repair hundreds of Jewish headstones vandalized in St. Louis and Philadelphia.

"Putting our religious differences or even your political differences aside, the core of all of us is that we have a shared humanity," Mr. El-Messidi said in an interview. "We really wanted to reach out as human beings to help."

MICHAEL HENNINGER FOR THE NEW YORK TIMES

A memorial on Monday outside the Tree of Life Synagogue in Pittsburgh, where 11 people were fatally shot on Saturday. Several groups, including two Muslim organizations, have helped raise money for the victims.

In the hours after a gunman opened fire inside the Tree of Life synagogue, telling the police that he "wanted all Jews to die," there was an outpouring of support, within Pittsburgh and beyond, for the victims and their families.

It has served as a reminder of what Fred Rogers, the famed children's television host who lived within walking distance of the synagogue, said about tragedies: "Always look for the helpers. There are always people who are helping."

Blood banks in Pittsburgh kept their doors open late. Thousands of people attended vigils across the city, standing shoulder to shoulder in the cold rain with people of many faiths. Stores donated food. And the Pittsburgh Penguins hockey team, which organized a blood drive on Monday, will collect money from fans before Tuesday night's game.

At an interfaith vigil on Sunday evening, Rich Fitzgerald, the top county official in Pittsburgh, spoke about how he had watched people snap into action after the shooting, organize assistance efforts and offer whatever help they could.

"We saw a coming together of people all over this community and all over this region," Mr. Fitzgerald said at the vigil, held at Soldiers and Sailors Memorial Hall. "Bigotry will not win. Hatred will not win."

One person who jumped at the chance to help was Shay Khatiri, an Iranian-American who immigrated to the United States four years ago. Mr. Khatiri, who lives in Washington, created a GoFundMe campaign for the synagogue on Saturday.

Over the weekend, donors contributed more than $100,000. Then $200,000. And by Tuesday evening, the campaign had raised nearly $900,000. The latest goal is to bring in $1 million.

Among the donors, "there are Steins and Bergs, and there are Mohammeds. There are generic American names, and there are Asian ones," Mr. Khatiri wrote on GoFundMe. "It is only fitting that Americans of all backgrounds — immigrant, native-born, Jewish, atheist, Buddhist, Hindu, Christian, Muslim, etc. — are uniting against this hateful act. America is beautiful!"

Mr. El-Messidi said his fund-raiser started to distribute some of the donations on Monday morning. He hopes to raise enough to cover the funeral costs of those who were killed and medical bills for those who were hospitalized.

He said his mind has returned again and again to the story of Prophet Muhammad, the founder of Islam, when he saw a funeral procession for a Jewish man. The prophet stood up to pay his respects. When his disciples next to him noted that the man was not a Muslim, Muhammad replied, "Was he not a soul?"

Mr. El-Messidi said that while Judaism and Islam have their differences, they were linked by a tragic similarity: Followers of both faiths have been targeted in bigoted attacks. "The shared discrimination has brought both communities closer," he said.

CHAPTER 4

Health Care, Memorials and the Personal Campaign

In recent years, the personal crowdfunding campaign has gained significant traction. Those seeking funds for their personal medical care, the memorial service of a loved one or on behalf of a homeless person in need have turned increasingly to crowdfunding for a solution, sharing the circumstances with the public and asking for support. How to decide which situations are most dire, or those causes most worthy of support, makes this area of crowdfunding one often marked by controversy.

Medical Care, Aided by the Crowd

BY NICOLE LAPORTE | APRIL 13, 2013

TWO YEARS AGO, Chase Adam, a Peace Corps volunteer in Costa Rica, was riding a bus through a town called Watsi, when a woman got on board asking for money. Her son, she said, needed medical attention and she couldn't pay for it. As the woman walked through the bus, she showed people a copy of her son's medical record. Mr. Adam, who is now 26, noticed that nearly everyone donated money.

The experience gave him an idea.

"I thought it'd be really cool if there was a Kiva for health care," he said, referring to the crowdfunding Web site that allows donors to provide microloans to entrepreneurs in developing countries.

Over the next several months, he devoted his free time to creating a business plan for an online start-up that he named after the town where he got the idea. Watsi, which started last August, lets people donate as little as $5 toward low-cost, high-impact medical treatment for patients in third-world countries.

The procedures range from relatively simple ones like fixing a broken limb to more complicated surgery — say, to remove an eye tumor. But the treatments generally have a high likelihood of success and don't involve multiple operations or long-term care.

Operated out of an apartment in Mountain View, Calif., Watsi works with nonprofit health care providers in 13 countries, including Cambodia, Nepal, Guatemala and Ethiopia. The providers identify patients meeting Watsi's criteria; the providers themselves have been vetted by Watsi and its medical advisory team, which includes Dr. Mitul Kapadia, director of the physical medicine and rehabilitation program at Benioff Children's Hospital of the University of California, San Francisco, and a half-dozen other doctors and medical professionals.

The profiles of the patients are posted on the Watsi site, and the online community begins donating. Medical care is given when the health partners decide that it is "medically appropriate," Mr. Adam said. Sometimes that care is given before money is raised on Watsi, and the profile remains on the site so that fund-raising can continue. Watsi maintains an operational reserve for this purpose, he said.

Watsi represents the next generation of charities dependent on online donors, evolving the model started by sites like Kiva. With just a few mouse clicks, Kiva users, say, are able to lend money to a restaurant owner in the Philippines — and to examine her loan proposal and repayment schedule, to read about her and see her photograph.

Charities have long recognized the importance of photographs and narratives in soliciting donations. Watsi's Web site, too, shows vivid images of its patients, and tells their stories. For example, a 9-year-old girl in Myanmar who needs eye surgery has had to miss a year of school because of her condition.

"People like to feel like their donation is making a difference to an individual," said Timothy Ogden, managing director of the Financial Access Initiative at New York University's Robert F. Wagner Graduate School of Public Service. "That's how they like to give — where there's a face and a personal connection."

While Kiva offered pictures and much more from the start, information about its own operations was not always easy to find on its site. In 2009, when donors learned that loans weren't going directly to the people in need but to microfinancing institutions that had already made the loans, there was an uproar.

Even though the model makes sense — microfinancers play an important role in vetting individuals, and by giving them a loan upon request, the borrower does not have to wait weeks or months for money to be raised online — Kiva was criticized for a lack of transparency. It has since clarified how it works.

The kerfuffle pointed out how much information the public demands in the Internet age, particularly when it comes to nonprofit groups, where "the general public is skeptical," Mr. Adam said.

As a result, organizations like Watsi are trying to extend their microlending transparency to themselves. On Watsi's Web site, there is a Google Doc — an online document that can be shared by various approved users, and updated in real time — that lists details like the name of the doctor providing care, whether that care was delayed for any reason, a screen shot of the PayPal funds transfer, and whether the treatment was successful. The document also shows Watsi's monthly financial statement, which lists the cost of office supplies, salaries and travel expenses. If any problems occur during or because of treatment, donors are notified by e-mail.

Mr. Adam said his approach was partly in response to the Kiva controversy. But he said he found inspiration in other nonprofits like Nyaya Health, a nongovernmental organization started by Yale graduates that provides free health care in Nepal. Nyaya, which is a Watsi medical partner, has a health wiki that lets people upload the organization's monthly financial reports and minutes from internal meetings.

"I think there's a new batch of these nonprofits starting to emerge," Mr. Adam said. "They're dedicated to helping people understand how things work."

Not that this makes everyone comfortable. After one patient who received funding from Watsi did not survive surgery, some health care partners were "a little spooked," Mr. Adam said, given that the doctor's name was listed on the Watsi site. "Doctors don't want their names to be associated with failure," he said, adding that as a result of that, some medical partners briefly stopped approving riskier treatments as a way to avoid more undesirable outcomes.

And when Watsi began publishing its financial statements, the chief financial officer "was very scared," Mr. Adam said. "He was like: 'What if I made a mistake? People are going to crucify me!' "

People did find a few minor mistakes, as it turned out. "They e-mailed us, and we solved the situation in five minutes," Mr. Adam said. "What we've found is that by being transparent, we're actually crowdsourcing a lot of our work." In effect, the public is "reviewing all our financials, which is fantastic," he said.

But is a Google Doc enough to make donors feel confident about a group's credibility? "Certainly, I don't think it hurts," Mr. Ogden said. "But do we know that the data they're providing is true?"

"We have a big problem in nonprofit data circles in general about the quality of data," he said, because "the rules for accounting for nonprofits are so lax."

Mr. Adam says such concern is precisely why his organization shows monthly statements line by line. "We provide much more detail about how things actually are working, and specific costs, such as Web hosting and salaries," he said. "You see some of that on 990 tax forms, but not nearly to the degree of resolution that we have."

WATSI recently participated in an incubator program at Y Combinator, which provides start-ups with seed money along with mentoring. So far, Watsi has raised about $200,000, which has paid for treatment of more than 270 patients.

But as those numbers grow, providing detailed information about each patient and his or her care could prove difficult. Dr. Paul Polak, a social entrepreneur and author of "Out of Poverty," said that much detail was possible in a small operation with few patients, but he asked: "How are you going to do that when you have 50,000?"

Mr. Adam says Watsi is becoming more streamlined. It is developing a system to let its care providers upload patient information directly to a central database. Currently, Watsi enters that data manually into the Google Doc.

Before entering the Y Combinator program, Watsi was paying for an average of three patients a week. Since completing the program, that average is now 17 a week. And three months ago, Mr. Adam and his two full-time co-workers started receiving a salary. (Mr. Adam makes about $45,000 a year.)

"Honestly, that's been the biggest milestone so far, with regard to us personally," he said.

"When I got that first paycheck, despite it being pretty small, I remember thinking that I couldn't believe I was being paid to do something I love so much."

Managing Health Costs With Crowdfunding

BY CONSTANCE GUSTKE | JAN. 30, 2015

SOMETIMES PAYING FOR a loved one's health care expenses literally takes a crowd.

Norm Breyfogle, a comic book artist known for his work on Batman, found himself struggling after a stroke in December. He had no health insurance. He was partly paralyzed on his left side, unable to use his valuable drawing hand. And Mr. Breyfogle, 54, was in a nursing home in the Upper Peninsula of Michigan, facing months of physical therapy.

Worried about his brother's rapidly rising bills, Kevin Breyfogle decided to step in. He started a crowdfunding campaign, which raises small donations from donors, on the site YouCaring.

"We had to come up with something really quick," Kevin Breyfogle said, adding that crowdfunding worked better than he imagined. His crowdfunding team set a goal of $200,000 to pay for his brother's continuing care, raising $20,000 in the first day.

As more caregivers face paying for loved ones' unexpected out-of-pocket health care costs, they are turning to crowdfunding sites that focus on personal causes like Mr. Breyfogle's. Sites like GiveForward, GoFundMe and Fundly have devoted sections to health expenses, including specific diseases like cancer.

Even the crowdfunding powerhouse Indiegogo has stepped into the personal crowdfunding arena with its introduction of Indiegogo Life, which includes medical fund-raising, in December.

High out-of-pocket health expenses can quickly deplete a sick person's financial resources. According to a 2014 Commonwealth Fund survey, 87 percent of people age 65 or older in the United States have at least one chronic illness. Despite Medicare coverage, though, older adults in the United States have more difficulty paying for their care

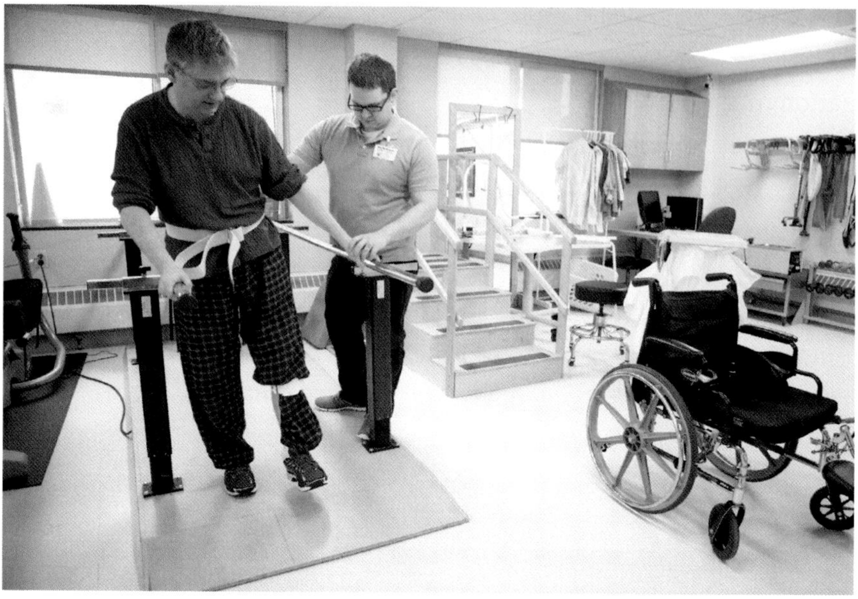

DANIELLE S. PEMBLE FOR THE NEW YORK TIMES

Norm Breyfogle, a comic book artist, working with Ben Butkovich, a physical therapist. After Mr. Breyfogle had a stroke, his brother raised money for his care through a crowdfunding campaign.

than peers in other developed countries, mostly because of out-of-pocket costs and limits to care, the survey found.

To fill the void, crowdfunding sites are stepping in, with people posting requests for donations to pay for funerals, out-of-pocket medical expenses and, sometimes, interim nursing home care.

The Chicago-based GiveForward, for example, has helped raise $149 million for crowdfunding campaigns since starting in 2008, said Ethan Austin, the organization's president and co-founder. And most of the money goes to meet unexpected medical expenses, he said. "No one should have to go through a difficult illness alone," he said, adding that more baby boomers are using it for parents' care. "And giving someone the opportunity to help is a big gift."

"Five years ago, no one would have crowdfunded expenses," Mr. Austin said. "But there's a tidal shift coming as health care expenses rise."

Caregivers worry most about financial concerns, said Brooks Kenny, executive vice president at Lotsa Helping Hands, an organization that offers resources to caregivers and volunteers in the Washington area. So crowdfunding can be a powerful solution, she added.

In a mobile society, crowdfunding can cast a big virtual net. Buckley Fricker, a geriatric care manager and president of Buckley's for Seniors, which offers nonmedical care to older people, said Americans no longer lived in communities where everyone helped take care of a sick elder. In its place, technology can pull from all areas of the country.

"Technology is breaking down solid walls with virtual windows," Ms. Fricker said. "And it can virtually recreate the family."

Don't expect to go back to the electronic money trough often, though. Fund-raising for unusual expenses works best, Ms. Fricker said. "The need for geriatric care is so far and wide that it's hard to draw out interest," she said. So crowdfunding is more successful with extraordinary circumstances, such as Mr. Breyfogle's.

"Infinite dragging on of expenses won't garner support," Ms. Fricker said. People want to visualize the difference they're making, such as outfitting a home with an elevator or buying a new wheelchair.

Once there's a specific need, building a wide network is crucial. Don't just rely on the biggest and best crowdfunding sites to help you, Ms. Fricker advised, but use emails and Facebook to pull in more donations. Mr. Breyfogle was able to draw on a fan base of 5,000 Facebook friends, but having friends spread the word to other friends helps too, experts said. They can even be friends from clubs, churches or schools. "Tap into your network communities where lots of people know each other," Ms. Kenny suggested.

"Crowdfunding is never going to be a platform where millions give," explained Mr. Austin. "Usually, 80 percent of the people who contribute are people you know rather than strangers. The key is getting people with big, active networks involved."

Start the process with closest friends and family to build momentum, he suggested.

"And realize that people don't always contribute the first time you ask," he said. "It may take three or four times of continued asking." Getting three or four people out of 100 to donate is a good rate, he said, adding that persistence is important.

The Pataki family turned to their friends and family to help pay for a health expense gap after Marguerite Pataki, a 76-year-old California resident who had a stroke last summer, was placed in at-home care rather than a nursing home, which health insurance would have covered.

"Suddenly costs started snowballing," said Monica Pataki, Marguerite's daughter, who lives in Arizona. "My dad was wading through a morass of bills and fees." And the Pataki children were quickly running out of money.

So the family started a fund-raising campaign on GiveForward in early December to raise $11,648 to pay for a caregiver and other expenses. "Within 15 minutes we were set up online," Ms. Pataki said. "Short of selling everything we have, this is the best thing we could come up with." To rev up the campaign, the Patakis sent out dozens of emails.

One of the donors was Marlene Robinson, who lives in California and knows the Patakis. Ms. Robinson, who believes in paying favors forward, made a small donation. "I want to support campaigns I resonate with," said Ms. Robinson, a self-employed inventor. "It's about connecting with things that feed a purpose."

Asking for small contributions increases the chances of getting participation, Ms. Fricker said, and the various crowdfunding sites usually allow donations starting at a dollar.

At the heart of any good campaign is a compelling story, though. So adding lots of photos and detailed information about the loved one can increase donations, experts say. The Patakis ultimately added six more photos to their crowdfunding campaign page. Adding video, even taken with a cellphone, can add more personal color. "You can raise 150 percent more with a video," said Danae Ringelmann, a co-founder of Indiegogo.

Older, less technologically adept donors may balk at giving money online, though. So the Patakis called some elderly family friends on the phone. "Speaking to them works better," Ms. Pataki said. "And they've been kind and sent checks."

The family had to overcome some discomfort about asking for money, Ms. Pataki acknowledged.

"You're laying out your dirt online," she said. "And it's humiliating." As the campaign evolved, however, the Patakis found that donors were touched by their mother's story rather than pitying their lack of money.

Crowdfunding can be an excellent way to bring in money that's tax-free. The I.R.S. treats these personal-cause donations as gifts for recipients, Mr. Austin noted.

Fund-raisers may need to spend money to make money, though. Some personal crowdfunding sites charge fees for their services. GiveForward, for example, charges a 7.9 percent fee plus 50 cents per donation transaction.

For Mr. Breyfogle, though, crowdfunding has become the difference between hope and despair. Although the campaign continues for another month, "I don't feel that I'm in dire financial straits anymore," he said.

In Defense of the Personal Crowdfunding Campaign

BY RON LIEBER | NOV. 20, 2015

"I CAN'T EVEN BELIEVE I'm writing this, or asking for this, but this is the reality."

This appeal on GoFundMe appeared on Monday, like thousands of others showing up each day on that site and others like it. The Nowakowski siblings of Milwaukee were asking for $25,000 to help their parents, as their father struggled to pay for the care of their mother, who has dementia and mobility challenges and recently moved into an assisted-living home.

Their biggest goal is a wheelchair-accessible van to restore some sense of normalcy to their parents' lives, allowing them to continue

DARREN HAUCK FOR THE NEW YORK TIMES

The siblings Luke and Dana Nowakowski started a campaign on GoFundMe to raise $25,000 to help their father pay for the care of their mother, who has dementia and mobility challenges.

going to the farmers' market and to see their favorite band, the Whiskey Belles.

The family's situation is not life or death, or even as severe as imminent eviction or lack of electricity, like some of the requests on older sites like Modest Needs.

But it's not in the same category as art projects or entrepreneurial ventures either, such as those you'd see on Kickstarter. Charitable fund-raising campaigns or requests for race-for-the-cure pledges are a different type of plea, too.

Instead, the increasing number of personal appeals like this represent a muddled middle, where people who do not have enough ask for help to make life better. The requests lie somewhere along the murky wants-versus-needs continuum, but it would be hard to agree on exactly where they sit.

We are not used to this, the sheer nakedness of people putting a number to their problems and disclosing it to the world. But more financial transparency is almost always better than less, and the Internet provides an emboldening platform. Then, it is up to everyone to push the button to give money or not.

Plenty of people are making the requests. GoFundMe plays host to about 3,300 new personal campaigns (as the company refers to them) each day. The most common category is medical expenses, followed by memorials and funerals, general emergencies and education costs.

While not all requests are successful, people can keep whatever they take in, even if they don't hit their goal (and also if they exceed it). As of September, the askers had raised over $1 billion in the previous 12 months, though the for-profit company does take about 8 percent in fees for customers in North America. The money it transfers for personal campaigns is a gift, so the givers get no tax deduction, and the company does not guarantee that people are telling the truth. It urges people to give money only to those they "know and trust."

So who are these people who are giving and taking?

There is something appealing about the idea that this is "really Midwestern," as a writer for the personal finance website The Billfold suggested earlier this year. Indeed, to the money-talk-isn't-polite crowd, crowdfunding is often something to sneer at. But those of us reared far from moneyed coastal communities keep right on with our barn raisings, virtual or otherwise.

It apparently isn't always easy to figure out just how bold to encourage people to be, though. One service called Present Value began as a registry where engaged couples could just ask directly for cash in lieu of upgraded kitchen appliances and more traditional wedding gifts. The platform is still there, but the company has shifted its focus toward helping users figure out how to put the money they receive to work, whether in stocks or college savings.

Those gift requests were strictly wants. Other kinds of requests that are further down the necessity continuum began appearing on sites like Indiegogo a few years ago and complicated the proceedings. Yet it didn't make much sense for users to see requests for help with something like fertility treatments next to fledgling art projects in need of money.

Plus, the branding was all wrong. "Indie" suggests filmmaking, and "go go" suggests movement and dancing, not eggs and sperm that are having trouble meeting — let alone funeral expenses or missed college tuition payments. Indiegogo has now moved the more acute financial requests to Generosity.com.

One advantage that all such sites offer is that you don't have to look anyone in the eye when making your request. You can ask everyone without having to ask anyone in particular. It's also less aggressive than making a one-on-one plea.

Or perhaps it's just passive-aggressive. There is always the possibility that the person who is asking is making a list and checking it twice (and then 50 times more) to see who has pitched in and who has not. But Dana Nowakowski, who made the van appeal with her brother, Luke, said that she was not doing that at all.

"I dreaded doing it," she said. "I've been writing it in my head every morning for the last couple of weeks, in the shower, getting ready, just dreading writing this story."

So why do it? "There is an element of desperation," she said. Hers, she explained, is a family that does not ask for things. They work for what they get and they buy what they can afford and that's just how it has always been. They do not expect things or feel entitled to them.

But her parents, she said, had done so much for so many people for so long, baking cookies and making casseroles and giving rides and handing out gift cards. Her father is a retired teacher. And few people knew just how desperate things had become in recent weeks, when her mother moved into the dementia care home and the costs became clear. "They were the first ones there for friends and family," she said. "So I guess I kind of thought, 'Hey, it's their turn. It's time for everyone to return the favor.' "

In an odd coincidence, Ms. Nowakowski works as a writer for an ad agency. So was this just another "campaign," as GoFundMe puts it, except one where she had to sell her family's plight? "Selling implies exaggerating, calculating, sometimes even manipulating the truth," she said. "The sad truth is I didn't have to sell anything. This crappy situation sells itself."

Even introducing the idea of commerce here, however, ought to make us all deeply uncomfortable. Is this what we've been reduced to, weighing pitches for charity from people we know and pitting them against strangers online, or the needy whom more traditional charities serve?

What was I to make of my own cynicism as I found myself deep in the weeds on these sites this week, evaluating a newly fatherless child. Should I support her, given that I was pretty sure that a seven-figure settlement would be coming her way because of the circumstances of her father's accidental death?

So here's another way to think about these sites. They don't replace traditional charity, or obviate the obligation to vote and lobby for policy changes that could reduce many of the needs they serve. But they can allow you to honor your own family's history of having been helped by letting you pay back those who have supported you in the past, or toss the rope to others who are in circumstances similar to ones that you once found yourself in.

That, at least, is how family, friends and fans of the Nowakowskis seem to be seeing it. As of this writing, they've raised $20,830, more than 80 percent of their goal. And Ms. Nowakowski said she didn't feel a shred of regret.

"The support we're getting from this is just as important to me as the money," she said. "You can really feel the love, the warmth, the fact that people have your back. And that's what we needed the most."

How a Homeless Teenager's Viral Story Caused a Battle Over GoFundMe Money

BY KATIE ROGERS | JULY 26, 2016

WHEN A HOMELESS TEENAGER named Fred Barley rode a bicycle some 50 miles into Barnesville, Ga., this month, he set up a small tent in a clump of bushes near Gordon State College, where he had registered. When two police officers found him, he told them he wanted to get a job before classes started.

Two police officers checked the 19-year-old into the Sun Inn nearby for a couple of nights, paying out of their own pockets, the motel's owner, Ansuya Pandya, said in an interview. That good deed caught the attention of another resident, Casey Blaney, who fired up a GoFundMe page and paid to extend Mr. Barley's stay.

"I thought that helping find him a job, giving him some money and paying for his motel was going to be it for me," Ms. Blaney wrote on the Success for Fred campaign page. "I just couldn't stop thinking about how lonely and rejected he must feel."

Mr. Barley's story, reported in The Atlanta Journal-Constitution and WSBTV, an Atlanta TV station, was spun out onto news sites across the internet, and had all the ingredients of a viral feel-good tale. Mr. Barley told reporters he had ridden his younger brother's bike six hours into town from Conyers, Ga., but little else is known about his life.

Still, his living conditions in Barnesville tugged at the heartstrings of many. Ms. Blaney's campaign became amplified by the breathlessly emphatic nature of social media after the story was posted on a popular Facebook page called Love What Matters. The support quickly poured in — $15 here, $20 there — from people across the world. And the campaign gathered more than $184,000 in 12 days.

Then, Ms. Blaney abruptly halted fund-raising last week. The pendulum of social media support had swung back to skepticism and suspicions about where the money was going. Now, weeks after the story began, it has devolved into a cautionary tale about the nature of online fund-raising and the perils of being a good Samaritan in the digital age.

'HE'S A 19-YEAR-OLD KID. HE'S OVERWHELMED.'

Two weeks after Mr. Barley came to Barnesville, he has gone into hiding after being accused of taking the money and running, even though no funds have been dispersed from the campaign. Ms. Blaney is lying low, as well, after being accused of also taking the money. She is speaking only through a lawyer, Wright Gammon, who did not answer phone and email requests for comment on Monday.

"The only person getting hands on the money is Fred if he's in school and the trustee that's going to make the decisions as to when and how much to pay," Mr. Gammon told The Atlanta Journal-Constitution last week.

Ms. Blaney insisted on the campaign's Facebook page Friday, "All of the funds are going into an educational trust."

She also told of the toll of handling the campaign, writing, "I am a wife and a mother and cannot continue to handle the multitude of calls, texts, social media requests and comments."

On Tuesday, GoFundMe said in a statement: "We are working with both Fred and Casey on the transfer of funds. The funds won't be transferred to a trust until all parties come to an agreement. Over all, it's important to remember that the money will go directly to Fred's education."

The episode has divided residents of Barnesville, a small town of 6,500 in Lamar County where rumors tend to spread fast online, according to Debbie Adamson, the owner of DB's Pizzeria, who said she had reached out to Mr. Barley with a job offer.

He worked at the pizzeria for a week and a half as a dishwasher and a pizza-making trainee before telling Ms. Adamson about an offer for free tuition at another college in Alabama. He later called saying that the offer didn't pan out, and Ms. Adamson has not heard from him since Friday, she said.

"Right now he has more or less gone into hiding mode," Ms. Adamson, 53, said in an interview on Monday. "No one has seen or heard from him. He's a 19-year-old kid. He's overwhelmed."

Messages sent to Mr. Barley on Facebook were not immediately answered. A Facebook page listed under his name appears to show that he has commented on a financial trust: "I DO NOT AND I REPEAT DO NOT CONSENT to the trustee committee they have established. I have not spoken to her lawyer," he wrote. In another post, Mr. Barley wrote that he hadn't received any of the money.

It is unclear if Mr. Barley will meet his original goal of attending Gordon State. A public information officer for the school, Tamara Boatwright, said in an interview, "All I'm saying about Mr. Barley at this time is that he is registered for fall semester and that he has applied to live on campus."

'THE SCOPE OF THESE THINGS CAN QUICKLY GROW'

Explaining the dynamics at play when stories of tragedy or triumph over adversity hit the internet's bloodstream, Cody Switzer, an assistant managing editor with The Chronicle of Philanthropy, said that an observer's first instinct is to want to give money in any way possible to help.

But, Mr. Switzer said, individuals who start online fund-raising campaigns are often unprepared for the media attention, and the viral nature of those campaigns can sometimes fail to address greater issues faced by people who are economically vulnerable, like poverty or homelessness.

"The scope of these things can quickly grow in a way that doesn't necessarily get at a structural problem," Mr. Switzer said. "It solves a short-term need for an individual, but it doesn't always address larger problems."

In addition, he added, when large sums of money are raised online, the distribution is often more complicated than one individual can handle. (Sometimes, several campaigns compete at once. Some 300 GoFundMe campaigns raised $6.2 million for the victims of the recent mass shooting at a nightclub in Orlando, Fla., that killed 49 people.)

GoFundMe recommends that donors give money only to people they personally know and trust, and warns that campaign pages may not all have accurate information. While a number of campaigns have been successful, raising large sums of money using social media as the main tool can spur questions about where, exactly, is the money going.

One of the platform's most successful campaigns was started in 2013, when Glenn O'Neill and his wife, Cara, began a GoFundMe campaign that raised over $2 million to search for a cure for their daughter, Eliza, and other children who had a metabolism disorder called Sanfilippo Syndrome.

The O'Neills created a nonprofit organization and tried to be transparent about where the funds were going, but still encountered questions from donors.

"A lot of times people don't read the detail of what exactly is happening," he said of GoFundMe campaigns, adding, "People will always have questions."

In Mr. Barley's case, a campaign set up by a stranger has divided a small group of people who were trying to help someone they did not know. Most of those people, Ms. Adamson said, have retreated.

"It's just funny because I'm the only one who will answer my phone now," Ms. Adamson said. She added: "It's an interesting story about how and what can happen in the long run if things aren't done correctly."

She said the job offer for Mr. Barley still stands — if he returns to Barnesville.

Crowdfunding a Well-Deserved Break

BY TEJAL RAO | APRIL 25, 2017

I HAD HOPED READERS would enjoy following a food vendor around on the streets of Manhattan for a day, but I hadn't expected the story I wrote about Kabir Ahmed to take on a life of its own.

Mr. Ahmed, 46, immigrated from Bangladesh 23 years ago and now works five or six days a week selling chicken biryani and other hot dishes out of a halal food cart in the Financial District. The job is difficult and unglamorous, like many jobs in the food industry. It does not pay well.

Mr. Ahmed's wife had mentioned to him, in passing, the idea of saving up for a family cruise in the Caribbean. It was a luxury that Mr. Ahmed knew they could not afford for their family of six, but for some reason it had stuck with him.

"Have you been on a cruise?" he'd asked me on the day I spent reporting with him. "What is it like?" At the end of my article (which ran in the Food section on April 19), I wrote about Mr. Ahmed's longing to go on vacation.

Not long after my piece was published, readers sent emails asking how they could be helpful. I suggested they buy lunch at food carts, and tip well, especially on rainy days when business slows down. I also proposed learning more about the Street Vending Modernization Act, the New York legislation introduced last fall that would lift the cap on food vending permits, which Mr. Ahmed strongly supports.

Then one reader, Jennifer Nelson, started a crowdfunding campaign to raise money for Mr. Ahmed and his family and their dream vacation.

Ms. Nelson, a general manager at Buttermilk Channel, a restaurant in Brooklyn, read the article on Wednesday and posted it to Facebook. "I wrote a comment about how I wish I had money to buy this family a vacation," she said. "Immediately, people started commenting that they wished they did too."

AN RONG XU FOR THE NEW YORK TIMES

Kabir Ahmed takes a break outside his food cart after the lunchtime rush.

Ms. Nelson did a quick search for Caribbean cruises to estimate the cost for a family of six. Then she started a GoFundMe campaign and set the goal at $3,000. "I hope they can do something that might have seemed a little out of reach before," she said.

Many readers felt a connection to Mr. Ahmed, who is one of more than 10,000 people, most of them immigrants, who make a living selling food on the city's sidewalks. But when I first asked him if I could follow him around for a story in the paper, he was surprised. "A story about me?" he'd asked.

I explained that it would involve my pestering him all day with questions, but that in the end people might get to know him a little and understand what it's like to work as a vendor. He said O.K.

When I showed up at his house in Queens, Mr. Ahmed opened the door for me and a photographer, An Rong Xu, clearing toys and snack wrappers from his sofa to make space for us. He opened a box of kaju halwa, a soft, buttery sweet made from cashew nuts, as if we were family. I had to keep reminding him that I was working, too, and he didn't have to worry about taking care of me.

"Writing stories is a job?" he'd said, teasing me.

At the end of the day, after hopping in and out of his 10-foot-long metal cart a hundred times, jotting down notes on his recipes and watching a series of cute dog videos together, Xu and I both felt lucky to be reporting a story about Mr. Ahmed. "It was like spending a day with my own father," Xu wrote to me.

This past Friday, a couple of weeks after I had spent that day with Mr. Ahmed, I stopped by his cart to show him that the GoFundMe campaign for his family had reached over $5,000. "I cannot believe this, I cannot," he said.

Since the article was published, Mr. Ahmed's cart has been extra busy, he told me, and everyone seemed to know his name. His wife liked the story very much, he said, and his customers seemed to like it, too. But I wanted to know what Mr. Ahmed thought about it.

"My son liked the story," he said. As we shared a doughnut, it occurred to me that Mr. Ahmed hadn't read the piece.

"I started to read it on the train," he promised me, "but then I fell asleep. You know, Tejal, I was very tired."

Donations Will Help Former Tennis Prodigy Get Career-Saving Surgery

BY DAVID WALDSTEIN | OCT. 23, 2017

LAST WEEKEND Tornado Alicia Black traveled to a junior tennis tournament in Orlando, Fla., as the coach of a 10-year-old player. She hopes it was her last coaching job for the next 15 years.

The next time she goes to a tournament, perhaps in six months, Black expects to be playing.

A onetime prodigy whose playing career was halted two years ago by a hip injury she could not afford to fix, Black has received financial donations in recent weeks to pay for an operation and the six-month rehabilitation necessary to get back on the women's professional tennis tour.

SCOTT MCINTYRE FOR THE NEW YORK TIMES

Tornado Alicia Black, 19, could not afford the hip operation needed to continue her tennis career. After receiving tens of thousands of dollars in donations, she will have the surgery Tuesday.

She will have surgery on Tuesday to repair both of her hips. "From that point on," she said, "I'm a player again."

Black, 19, was once a rising star in American tennis, a runner-up in the 2013 United States Open junior girls' tournament. But in late 2015 her hip gave way, and she had surgery to repair a torn hip labrum. It never healed properly, though. Unable to play and earn money on tour, she began giving lessons to make a living.

The cost of the operation this week and of the rehabilitation was mostly covered by one donor: Alan Hassenfeld, the former chief executive of the Hasbro toy company, who read about her financial difficulties in an article in The New York Times.

Another donor, the author Steven Gillis, paid Black's outstanding $1,800 orthodontist bill. Black had not seen an orthodontist in more than a year because she could not afford to pay her bill. Thanks to Gillis, she recently had her braces removed.

Black also raised $40,180 in a little over a month through an internet crowdfunding campaign. She thought that would cover the cost of her surgery and rehab. But the operation alone turned out to be roughly four times as expensive as she had expected, about $62,000.

"I feel so blessed and I am so grateful to everyone," she said. "I originally didn't want to do the GoFundMe campaign. But a woman contacted me and said I should do it because if I got back on the tour and became successful, I could do so much for other people. That's my goal now."

A member of the International Tennis Hall of Fame's executive board, Hassenfeld runs his family's philanthropic foundation. He checked with people he knew to make sure Black was a worthy recipient of his donation.

"I don't usually give to individuals, but I was so moved by her story," he said. "I asked her to make two promises. One, that if she is ever able, she helps another tennis player in need. And two, that she invites me to her player box at the U.S. Open."

This month, using some of the money from the crowdfunding effort,

SCOTT MCINTYRE FOR THE NEW YORK TIMES

Black has been teaching tennis lessons to make money after the hip injury stalled her pro career.

Black traveled from her home in Delray Beach, Fla., to Philadelphia and met with two hip specialists. One will fix two sports hernias — tears in the lower abdominal muscles — and the other will shave down and repair structural damage to the pelvic bones.

"They said I made it a lot worse by coaching and waiting to have it done," Black said. "Originally, I thought I had one injury. It turned into four."

But she said the doctors had assured her that she should be able to get back on the court and resume her career at full strength after a six-month rehabilitation, which will begin in Philadelphia the day after her operation. Black will stay in a hotel there for two weeks and then return home to Florida.

She will use some of the crowdfunding money to cover the extra cost of the operation, beyond what Hassenfeld provided. She said she would use the remaining money to pay for a strength and conditioning coach, rent, utility bills, food and other expenses while she rehabilitates.

Black plans to be back on tour by next summer. She will have to rebuild her ranking, which was No. 404 at the time of her injury, and will aim to break into the top 100, where players start to earn enough money to make tennis a real livelihood.

If she succeeds in her comeback, Black said, she wants to open her own charity and address issues that have affected her life, like childhood homelessness. Black has said that she lived in homeless shelters with her family when she was young and that she also lived out of the family car for weeks at a time when she was 12.

"No child should ever have to go through that," she said. "I hope I can be in a position to help."

Because her family used food stamps, childhood hunger is another issue dear to her, she said, as is the high cost of medical care.

"Someday I'd like to be able to help a kid get an operation they can't afford," she said. "I think that would be a good way to pay everyone back for all their generosity to me."

Black said she was also interested in helping children get proper dental care. For the past several months, she said, she was embarrassed because she had the remnants of braces on her teeth. The wires were taken out, but she ran out of money before the attachments could be removed.

With help from Hassenfeld, Gillis and others, that is no longer a problem.

"I'm not embarrassed anymore," she said. "Now I can smile."

His Wife Died in the Santa Fe School Shooting. The World's Sympathy May Keep Him Alive.

BY DANIEL VICTOR | MAY 22, 2018

IN A GRIM LAYERING of American tragedies, a 67-year-old man with a lung disease was able to crowdfund his medical treatment only after his wife died in the Santa Fe, Tex., school shooting.

Cynthia Tisdale, 63, a substitute teacher at Santa Fe High School, was among the victims in Friday's shooting, in which a student used a shotgun and a handgun to kill eight students and two teachers.

She had hoped to one day retire and be a "full-time grandmother," said John Tisdale, her brother-in-law. "It will never happen."

Her husband, William Tisdale, was diagnosed with idiopathic pulmonary fibrosis, which leads to scarring of the lungs, making it harder to breathe. He was denied a lung transplant in December, when he was told he had 12 to 18 months to live, according to the family's GoFundMe page. Ms. Tisdale had taken the substitute teaching job partly to help pay his medical bills.

His family believed his best hope was an experimental stem cell treatment, which wasn't covered by insurance and would cost $13,000.

"With the procedure I have a chance for more time with your momma (my wife of 47 years), my children, and my wonderful grandchildren who I so much want to see grow up as much as possible," he said in a letter to his son that was posted on the GoFundMe page, which was created on March 29. "I fear without this I won't make it to see 2019."

The family initially got little support. The campaign had raised $1,215 from donors in six states as of May 18, more than $11,000 short of its goal.

Then the massacre in Santa Fe happened, and the world offered its sympathy to the family. As of Tuesday, donors had pledged more than $120,000, coming from all 50 states and at least 33 countries, according to Katherine Cichy, a GoFundMe spokeswoman.

In an interview on Tuesday, Mr. Tisdale said that he was overwhelmed by the support, and that there might now be enough money to afford a lung transplant, which had previously seemed too expensive. At the very least, he'll be able to afford the stem cell treatment.

"But I'd rather not," he said. "I'd rather have her. It isn't worth it."

Mr. Tisdale's son, William Tisdale Jr., said in an interview on Tuesday that the family has an appointment scheduled this week to get a second opinion on whether he would be a viable candidate for a transplant, which he wasn't considered before.

Mr. Tisdale Jr. said the extra money would help the family hire home health care for his father, a role his mother had performed, and cover the costs of her funeral.

Mr. Tisdale said his wife had worked with special education students, happily taking their calls at night to help them prepare for exams. In addition to Mr. Tisdale's medical bills, she was working to support her daughter, whose home took on two feet of water during Hurricane Harvey.

"There was never a question whether she enjoyed the job or not," he said. "She adored it."

On Twitter, the intersection of the tragedies was grist for a lot of head-shaking. "This is the gofundme for the man with terminal cancer whose wife had to go back to work to pay for it and was murdered in school the other day," one person tweeted.

Another user replied: "We've condensed America down to one tweet."

As Funeral Crowdfunding Grows, So Do the Risks

BY LAURA M. HOLSON | JUNE 5, 2018

IN THE EARLY MORNING of May 27, Vinson Pierce had a heart attack and died in his sleep, leaving behind a wife, three children and more than 300 students in Comanche, Tex., where he was the principal at the local high school. The news traveled quickly in this Texas Hill Country town, which holds a yearly barbecue cook-off and antique car and tractor festival.

After getting word of Mr. Pierce's death, a co-worker set up a campaign on GoFundMe.com to raise money to help his widow pay for the funeral and other costs. Mr. Pierce, 35, did not have life insurance, explained Gary Speegle, the superintendent of the Comanche Independent School District. "We are a small, rural community, and when everyone heard what happened, they wanted to help," he said.

More than 1,000 people shared the GoFundMe campaign on Facebook, and it was featured by a local news station. In all, 276 people donated more than $25,000, a considerable sum. "Now they won't have to worry about funeral expenses," Mr. Speegle said. "It gives the family some space."

Crowdfunding campaigns are designed for just about everything these days: making video games; filming movies; paying for trips to Disney World; and, in a reflection of today's astronomical health care costs, covering medical bills. In recent years, too, campaigns have become popular among families and friends seeking emergency funds to cover burial and funeral costs for a loved one who has died.

GoFundMe, one of the largest fund-raising sites, says that 13 percent of its campaigns created in 2017 were described as memorials, which include funerals and are one of the company's fastest growing categories. That follows on a 2015 study by the Funeral and Memorial Information Council, which reported that 17 percent of adults aged

20 to 39 had used the internet to solicit or donate money for funeral-related arrangements.

There is little doubt consumers are interested in online funeral fund-raising. In April, GoFundMe acquired YouCaring.com, another popular charitable fund-raising site, which caters to the bereaved. "For many people, who have no other place to turn, we become the most important company to them," said Rob Solomon, the chief executive of GoFundMe.

Some funeral home directors, though, have begun asking relatives and friends to sign documents that relieve businesses of fault if a campaign goes awry, or funds are misrepresented or misused. Others, still, want to ensure they get paid.

"Our position is to suggest to people who are making choices to keep within their means," said R. Bryant Hightower Jr., a funeral director in Carrollton, Ga., and a board member of the National Funeral Directors Association. "We don't want people putting a number out there to profit."

And that has some critics wondering: Is crowdfunding the best way to pay for a funeral?

Joshua Slocum, the executive director of the Funeral Consumers Alliance, an advocacy group based in Burlington, Vt., said that crowdfunding might encourage funeral homes to upsell services to match the donation. He worries, too, that consumers are unprepared for the inevitable (we *are* talking about death here), lulled into thinking family and friends will be able to scrape together enough cash through donations after they are gone.

"This is an indication of where we are as a society," Mr. Slocum said. "We are seeing the modern equivalent of the carwash and bake sales."

Loved ones have always pitched in during a time of crisis; Mr. Speegle said residents of Comanche would have helped the Pierce family whether there was GoFundMe or not. The average cost of a traditional funeral and cremation is $6,260, according to the funeral association. A funeral and a burial can cost about $10,000.

What is different today, though, is that the number of people available to participate has expanded globally with social media. And that means successful campaigns — those that are shared widely on Facebook and Twitter — must have a compelling story to attract donors.

Mr. Solomon said his staff coaches funeral organizers on what angles to pursue to make a campaign go viral. "If a picture is worth 1,000 words, a video is worth 10,000 words," he said.

The bereaved, too, are advised to contact reporters and refresh pages with comments to maintain interest. "Local media matters to our campaigns," Mr. Solomon said. That's because if it doesn't resonate close to home, word is unlikely to spread. Indeed, many campaigns do not reach their target. Mr. Hightower said that about a third of the campaigns he had seen failed to reach their goals.

Some funeral home directors noted that consumers occasionally defy the rules. Jonathan Fisher, a funeral director at Fisher Funeral Chapel and Cremation Services in Lafayette, Ind., said he created his own crowdfunding site, FundTheFuneral.com, after clients did not pay for services with donations they solicited elsewhere online. "Families would lie about the amounts raised," he said. "Two different times people fooled me."

One family "physically showed me the money from a campaign that would be enough to cover the service," Mr. Fisher said. "Then they disappeared." Another time, he said, a couple solicited donations for the funeral of an infant, even though he performed the service at no cost, as he often does when a baby dies.

That happened to Mr. Hightower, too. "We didn't know about it until someone called and they asked where to send the money," he said. "We called the family and said, 'We don't want to be a party to that.' "

Mr. Solomon maintained that there is rarely fraud on GoFundMe and said that if there is, the company will contact law enforcement.

But a funeral director starting his own crowdfunding website is not the answer, either, said Mr. Slocum of the Funeral Consumer Alliance. For one, FundTheFuneral collects a 5 percent fee based on donations raised, along with a standard 2.9 percent credit transaction. FundTheFuneral, too, does not disclose Mr. Fisher's ownership stake on its website. "There is clearly potential for a conflict of interest," Mr. Slocum said.

Jeremy Spiering, Mr. Fisher's business partner, said they charged the fee solely to cover costs. "He's not pushing it for profit on the side," he said of his business partner.

GoFundMe, by contrast, dropped its 5 percent fee for personal fund-raising, including funerals, last year after being criticized in the wake of the California wildfires. Mr. Solomon of GoFundMe acknowledged that consumers had been displeased. "People wanted access to all their money," he said.

FuneralFundMe.com is the newest entrant in the funeral crowdfunding industry. It was founded in April by Kate MacDonald, 26, a former personal trainer who lives in Tulsa, Okla. She said her father was in the funeral home business. "If you go into a funeral home, people are dressed nice," she said. "I felt like there wasn't a fund-raising platform that could parallel that."

Ms. MacDonald is aiming her business mostly at funeral home directors who want to offer crowdfunding to their clients. She has highlighted six campaigns on FuneralFundMe, including one that said it had raised $21,379 for Kelsey Evans, a marathon runner from Tyler, Tex., who climbed Mount Kilimanjaro and died of breast cancer, leaving her family with $100,000 in medical bills. Ms. Evans is photographed hugging her dog.

There is one problem: The campaigns are fake.

Ms. MacDonald acknowledged that she created mock-ups to attract funeral home directors, but does not disclose that on her website. "We haven't had any real ones yet," she said. "I'm trying to teach directors what is an effective campaign."

When asked about it, Mr. Slocum sighed. "We've gotten to the point where the funeral home is the client," he said. "It's not the family."

Kip Zarse, a project manager at a construction company in Westpoint, Ind., said he was grateful for the $2,615 raised to help his family pay for his stepdaughter's funeral in January. Mr. Zarse worked with Mr. Fisher at FundTheFuneral. "Things were a little tight," he said. "We would have gotten by. But it was a nice gesture from the community."

"There were a few unknowns and anonymous folks," he said. "We did have one person who said, 'You don't know us, but someone helped us in our time of loss.' "

At 12, He Lost His Best Friend. He Found a Way to Remember Him.

BY MATT STEVENS | DEC. 12, 2018

KALEB HAD BIG PLANS for his best friend, KJ. To him, it was never a question of whether KJ would get out of the hospital; it was simply a question of when.

KJ, after all, had a history of battling a body that betrayed him: A flu shot made him sick when he was 13 months old; he learned he had leukemia shortly afterward; he had two bone-marrow transplants.

And yet KJ — Kenneth Gross Jr. — seldom complained.

"He was happy even though he went through all that stuff," observed Kaleb Klakulak, a 12-year-old of few words.

But years of chemotherapy and radiation ate away at KJ's most important organ. By age 9, he had developed congestive heart failure and by Jan. 7, 2018 — a few days after his 12th birthday — KJ was admitted to a hospital full time. He needed a heart transplant.

Kaleb, though, was undeterred. In his mind, when KJ was released, he and his mother would move north from Warren, Mich., to Romeo, Mich., where Kaleb and his family live. The two boys would reside blocks from each other, as they had when they met in the second grade.

On May 1, though, Kaleb's mother, Kristy Hall, took a phone call from KJ's mother; she had a bad feeling about the call, and her intuition proved correct.

"I remember walking back home," Ms. Hall said, "and thinking, 'How am I going to tell my son?' "

'BROTHERS, JUST OF A DIFFERENT RACE'

When Kaleb and KJ first met five years ago, they could not stop talking about each other and insisted on spending hours at each other's houses. Their mothers quickly understood why their sons got along.

Both were unusually quiet and were being raised by single mothers at the time. They even looked alike, according to KJ's mother, LaSondra Singleton.

"Fat cheeks," Ms. Singleton said. "I call them brothers, just of a different race."

Sometimes the boys put down their video games and spent a day at Greenfield Village — a collection of historic buildings — or saw a movie. Kaleb even invited KJ to come to his church, and KJ became a regular there who loved to sing.

It all ended early this year when KJ was hospitalized for the last time. He needed a new heart and was confined to the I.C.U., with a tube in his throat that prevented him from talking. He became depressed — and doctors turned to Kaleb for help.

Every Tuesday, for months, Kaleb and his mother would visit KJ. The boys would play a wrestling video game and would also paint. The boys did not have to communicate verbally, their mothers said. Kaleb would pick colors for KJ seemingly knowing what he wanted.

When 3 p.m. rolled around, KJ would extend his hand to pray. And on Wednesdays, Ms. Hall would FaceTime with KJ from church. Ms. Hall said KJ's favorite worship song was "10,000 Reasons," which she noted for its prescient verse.

And on that day
When my strength is failing
The end draws near
And my time has come
Still my soul will
Sing Your praise unending
Ten thousand years
And then forevermore
Forevermore

A VISIT THAT BECAME A GOODBYE

Ms. Singleton, 46, always knew her son was in for a long wait at the hospital. KJ had been exposed to many antibodies, so he would need just the right heart. In the meantime, doctors placed a device in his left ventricle hoping it would give him a better quality of life. "But it didn't work out that way," Ms. Singleton said.

She would regularly ask her son "if he wanted his heart." For a while, his written answer on a white board was, "Yes, Mama."

But in April, after more ups and downs, Ms. Singleton asked again.

"He didn't answer me," she said through tears. "He just gave me a long stare."

May 1 was a Tuesday, and Kaleb was getting ready to visit his friend.

When Ms. Hall texted Ms. Singleton to ask if KJ was up for it, however, Ms. Singleton called back — a signal, Ms. Hall said, that "something was wrong."

KJ had taken a turn. His mother was going to take him off life support. This visit would be a goodbye.

Ms. Hall explained the situation to her son the best way she knew how. But "he just kept looking at me," she recalled. "It was a very, very quiet drive."

That day, while KJ was still alive but not conscious, Kaleb cried and touched his friend's arm. There were other people in the hospital room, so Kaleb didn't say much.

HOW MUCH FOR A HEADSTONE?

KJ died that day. Ms. Singleton, a mother of six, had stopped working when her son last went into the hospital, and she remained unemployed in the first months after his death. She could not afford a headstone.

She mentioned this to Ms. Hall. Could she, perhaps, come up with a way to raise money for a marker?

Kaleb overheard his mother discuss the request and became curious. How much did a headstone cost? Whatever it was, it was more money than he had.

His first idea involved making KJ T-shirts and sending them to YouTube stars to ask for donations. Ms. Hall suggested something else: a PayPal donation site. Together, they decided not to simply ask for money; Kaleb would work for it.

He collected enough bottles and raked enough leaves to raise $250 — about half of his original goal. The PayPal post went up after Thanksgiving. Within days, Ms. Hall and her son showed up at Ms. Singleton's home with flowers, an apple pie and $900. The PayPal money, they hoped, would climb to $2,500 — enough, they thought, to buy the headstone.

"That just blew me away," Ms. Singleton said.

Then, last week, The Detroit News published an article about Kaleb's effort and the fund-raising campaign took off. As of Wednesday, the donation page said it had received more than 3,000 contributions — no odd jobs required.

Though the page said the $2,500 pledge goal had been met, it did not say how much money had been raised. Ms. Hall said she would disclose the amount only to Ms. Singleton. But she allowed that Ms. Singleton would end up with extra money.

For his part, Kaleb said he was happy that people were giving.

"Honestly, I'm just proud of him for doing what he should do — what everybody should do," Ms. Hall said. "We should help people we love."

In a telephone interview on Sunday, Ms. Singleton said she was not sure what she wanted her son's headstone to say. "I've procrastinated because it makes it final for me," she said.

The next evening, she went to select one. Ms. Hall and Kaleb accompanied her.

Asked on Tuesday whether she had decided what to inscribe, Ms. Singleton said she had:

KJ Gross

Cherished brother, son and friend

ANDREW R. CHOW contributed reporting.

CHAPTER 5

Controversy and the Future of Crowdfunding

Over the last decade, crowdfunding has become a popular method of reaching fund-raising goals for a diverse range of causes. As funding sourced from the community via the Internet is irrevocably tied to social media, innovations in technology and other rapidly changing entities, it seems inevitable that the landscape of crowdfunding will continue to shift and adapt. The articles in this chapter address how crowdfunding may attempt to overcome recent controversies and what challenges may arise in the future.

Why Would You Ever Give Money Through Kickstarter?

BY ROB TRUMP | FEB. 8, 2013

FOR ABOUT THREE YEARS, between the ages of 12 and 15, I spent much of my free time on Internet forums devoted to the collectible-card game Magic: The Gathering. It became an obsession, consuming my mind and becoming the only thing I wanted to talk about. And once I realized that nobody I ever met face to face was particularly interested in a long debate on the merits of Zuran Orb vis-à-vis Claws of Gix, I turned to the Web.

On one site in particular, I became a regular — not only in conversations about Magic rules and strategy but on general issues like

ILLUSTRATION BY TOM GAULD

politics, culture, science and sports. Over time, even as my interest in the game waned and I played less, my connection to the people I met stayed strong, and I was spending more and more time on the site. Many regulars and I became close friends. Yet my family was still freaked out when one community member, having decided to leave the game of Magic, sent me a huge box of his old cards.

When my mother found out that my mysterious benefactor by mail was a guy in his 20s, she immediately took the position that he was a child molester trying to lure me out to California from Minnesota. In all fairness, I have no evidence that he *wasn't* a predator, but the simpler explanation seems much more likely: he just wanted to give me a gift.

When a person is open and giving, our default reaction is often suspicion, especially when the Internet is involved. And it's exactly that sort of suspicion that has underscored much of the media reaction to Kickstarter, an online crowdfunding platform. More or less anyone is allowed to post a project on Kickstarter with a stated financing goal, and more or less anyone is allowed to contribute to that project. The major caveats are that the projects must be creative and that the creators must offer rewards at different tiers of contribution, much in the way that PBS offers you a tote bag if you donate a certain amount during a fund-raiser.

In the beginning, Kickstarter seemed primarily like a venue for upstart bands or small theater companies to raise a few thousand dollars to get projects off the ground. Over the past year, though, Kickstarter has played a surprising role in gathering increasingly astonishing amounts of money for increasingly well-known artists. In March 2012, the video-game auteur Tim Schafer sought $400,000 to make a new game but ended up with $3.36 million; in May, the musician Amanda Palmer set a goal of $100,000 to record a new album and raked in more than $1 million.

Along with a rise in the site's public profile, the media narrative about Kickstarter has changed from one of astonishment ("So, people will just give you money?") to one of skepticism ("All right, who's getting hosed here?") to the current uneasy middle ground — optimistic but ready to jettison the whole thing as soon as some opportunist abuses it to abscond with a bunch of cash. Kickstarter-financed projects that run into trouble or fail to materialize are often cited as a flaw in the model: to take only the two examples above, Schafer has documented for his backers that his project is on a pace to run over its budget, and Palmer, following her windfall, has faced criticism for soliciting free help from local musicians while on tour. The suggestion in both cases is that their Kickstarter contributors were somehow duped, like suckers who fell for a Nigerian e-mail scam.

The common thread in all of this coverage is that it typically uses the language and logic of simple supply and demand, regarding Kickstarter essentially as a meeting place for entrepreneurs and investors. Which is a big reason the site's success seems so hard to explain. Kickstarter, like the box of Magic cards I was given, is baffling by the tenets of a self-serving marketplace. ("What's in it for him?" was the question my mother was trying in vain to answer.) And if you allow for things like file-sharing — and many Kickstarter rewards and projects are the types of things that could be pirated, like games, albums or films — then it becomes fairly clear that pretty much none of the people donating have a purely economic incentive to participate at all. Why not just let everybody else finance this new album and download a torrent of it later?

But Kickstarter backers aren't investors, and they aren't looking for the project that will give them the greatest return on their money.

Kickstarter does not function as a store (as its Web site goes to great pains to remind you), any more than PBS is "selling" you a tote bag in exchange for your donation. Kickstarter as a phenomenon is made much more comprehensible once you realize that it's not following the logic of the free market; it's following the logic of the gift.

In his book "Debt: The First 5,000 Years," the anthropologist David Graeber examines our history of debt and money, concluding, in part, that humans do not naturally tend toward impersonal, reciprocal exchange. Instead, exchange usually develops in cultures first as a part of a larger social and cultural ritual. One of the most compelling cultures Graeber profiles is the Tiv of West Africa, who have very particular rules about exchange. For starters, they believe that bringing an economic transaction to full completion is essentially immoral, or at least frowned upon, because it implies that one party doesn't want anything to do with the other in the future. If a Tiv man or woman gives you a gift, you are supposed to respond with another gift of slightly greater or lesser value. The outstanding debt between the two of you is a signal that your relationship is going to continue. To respond with a gift of equal value would be to say implicitly that you wish to even things out and draw your relationship to a close.

Kickstarter is run according to a similar form of gift logic. The artists create a short video, explaining themselves and conveying their personality. People contribute to them because they're friends who know the artist personally; they're fans engaged in a highly personal if unidirectional relationship with the artist; or simply because they're intrigued by the project and want some sense of participation in it. (Though it has been estimated that only 10 to 20 percent of contributors find projects this way, through the Kickstarter site rather than through the artists' own social-media promotions — and on average, these people donate less money.)

In response to the contribution, as in Tiv custom, the artist gives something of slightly greater or lesser value to the person who contributed. And it's almost always the case that the rewards for donations have a lower market value than the money being asked for (much like that public-television tote bag). There's one notable reason for this: the highly personal logic of the gift exchange, a transaction by which a personal relationship is strengthened, not diminished.

There's also an odd symbiosis created by Kickstarter, a reversal of the way the culture industry traditionally operates. On Kickstarter, if not enough backers pony up, the project quite likely won't exist at all. This makes its projects oddly impervious to piracy. If all your potential fans are freeloaders inclined to download something only if it's free, your project won't be financed in the first place, and there will be nothing for them to pirate.

Some critics of Kickstarter have objected to the transaction fees collected by the site itself, which is the source of its revenue. Josh MacPhee, writing in The Baffler (for which Graeber often writes as well), complained that Kickstarter extracts value from social networks while giving nothing social in return.

Admittedly the interaction with Kickstarter Inc. is an impersonal, business transaction, but it's not an exploitative one: artists choose to use Kickstarter because it's a known entity, it adds some legitimacy to their projects and helps them with presentation. Communities flock to donate to Kickstarter projects for the same reasons. And it's not correct to say that Kickstarter gives nothing back. To the contrary, it provides something increasingly rare in today's society: a platform for an essentially noneconomic transaction, the kind that builds friendships and communities. Some of the more innovative users of Kickstarter, like Schafer, have even offered a kind of forum membership as a donation reward; an invitation into a place where fans can congregate and socialize online, much as I did in my early teenage years.

And unlike the individual projects featured on the site, Kickstarter, the business, is susceptible to market forces. If at some point we all decide that its fees are too high, there's nothing to stop people from migrating to any of Kickstarter's increasing number of competitors, like Indiegogo or RocketHub. Kickstarter is replaceable, in competition with other more-or-less-equivalent services, and it keeps no relationship with us after we've donated. We are free to leave it whenever we please.

In 1983, Lewis Hyde, another writer inspired by gift economies, published "The Gift," an examination of the nature of the creative impulse and its relationship to the market economy. Hyde emphasized the forward motion of the gift, arguing that artistic creation is propelled by eros, or love, rather than the logos of number-crunching, and as such it is incapable of being subsumed by the market. Even if art is sold, the forces that led to its existence operate according to the need to share something with the world. Hyde's focus on the artist as creator and gift-giver is narrower than Graeber's more historical approach, but it made "The Gift" a sensation and an inspiration to writers like Margaret Atwood and David Foster Wallace. And if Graeber's work helps us understand the psychology of crowdfunding, then Hyde's work is vindicated by Kickstarter's success. The desire to make art has always been inherently social, not economic, and now, even in a society defined by the free market, the means to produce art can come from an inherently social mechanism as well.

As with the Tiv, on Kickstarter, the reward gift doesn't bring the transaction to completion. After financing a project and dispensing rewards, artists who use Kickstarter are in a permanent debt to the fans who supported them. This is borne out by their actions: pretty much no one who has had a successful Kickstarter project has ever been able to shut up about how thankful they are. Many have subsequently donated to or helped promote other projects. And if the artists don't show the appropriate reverence for their benefactors, public opinion can turn nasty. The reaction against Palmer's use of others' volunteer labor occurred not because her call for free help indicated some maddening market inefficiency. (Unpaid labor, after all, is the height of efficiency.) What really upset people is that her actions seemed to indicate an insufficient appreciation for the gift she received.

Bonus Feature: Kickstarter by the Numbers

Total Projects Posted: 84,502

Total Projects Fully Financed: 35,405

Total Donations Since 2009: $470 million

Category With the Highest Success Rate: Dance (70.12%)

Lowest Success Rate: Fashion (27.42%)

Successfully Financed Projects That Raised More Than $1 Million: 20

Highest Total Amount Raised by One Project: $10,266,845 (Pebble E-Paper Watch)

Projects That Failed to Receive a Single Pledge: 9,265

Kickstarter-Financed Films That Appeared at the Sundance Film Festival in 2013: 17

Number That Won an Award: 5

(All statistics as of Jan. 29. From Kickstarter.com/help/stats.)

Celebrities With Their Hands Out

OPINION | BY JULIET LAPIDOS | SEPT. 14, 2013

SINCE 2009 THE crowdfunding Web site Kickstarter has matched artists and entrepreneurs struggling to finance creative projects with people on the Internet willing to contribute a little cash. The earliest adopters of the technology, on the pitching side, were small-time musicians, unestablished filmmakers and others with no clear access to capital.

Gradually, however, more prominent types have discovered the site. In March, Rob Thomas, creator of the TV series "Veronica Mars," and Kristen Bell, the star of the show, used Kickstarter to finance "Veronica Mars" the movie. They set a target of $2 million and ultimately brought in $5.7 million from more than 90,000 donors. In April, the actor-director Zach Braff raised $3.1 million for a follow-up to his 2004 directorial debut, "Garden State."

Over the summer Spike Lee, the two-time Academy Award nominee, took in $1.4 million for an untitled film about "human beings who are addicted to blood." And two weeks ago Maria Pinto, who designed a dress Michelle Obama wore at the 2008 Democratic National Convention, launched a Kickstarter campaign with a goal of reaching $250,000 for a new line of women's clothing.

Kickstarter, once the domain of unknowns seeking their first big break, is now also a resource for big names intrigued by the potential of micropatronage. Not surprisingly, this cultural shift has spurred howls of protest, with critical essays on celebrity "panhandling" washing over the media.

There are two main arguments against the celebrity invasion. First is that it's in poor taste for the rich-and-famous to solicit money from the public when they presumably have access to more traditional financing or might even be able to self-finance projects. The second is that, like affluent professionals descending on a cheap, hip neighborhood, celebrities are making Kickstarter less hospitable to aspiring artists. In May, the director Kevin Smith said he would never "suck any loot out of the crowdfunding marketplace that might otherwise go to a first-timer who can really use it."

The aversion to deep-pocketed stars on Kickstarter is understandable. But a big name does not guarantee access to financing for creative projects. Even established artists may struggle to attract investment — a point Mr. Lee made about his own experience in defending his decision to try crowdfunding. Besides, anyone who feels uncomfortable is under no obligation to give.

And contrary to what some believe, Kickstarter is not a zero-sum game. Instead of vacuuming up finite resources, celebrity campaigns seem to widen the donor pool. Forty-seven percent of Mr. Lee's backers had never before contributed on Kickstarter. Once drawn in by a celebrity, donors may patronize lesser-known artists. As the Kickstarter founders wrote on their blog in August, the "Veronica Mars" and Zach Braff bids "brought thousands of new people to Kickstarter who have since pledged more than $1 million to 6,000 other projects."

The gentrification of Kickstarter doesn't seem to be hurting its original inhabitants. It may even be helping them.

JULIET LAPIDOS is a staff editor for The New York Times Opinion section.

The Effect Crowdfunding Has on Venerable Nonprofits Raises Concern

BY ALINA TUGEND | FEB. 7, 2014

THE ADS RAN for years. The global charity Save the Children asked for a monthly donation, and in return, a few times a year the donors received a photo and handwritten note or drawing from children in impoverished places like Haiti.

The idea, of course, was that donors would have some sort of connection to the contribution. Most people knew that, in reality, the few dollars were not given directly to those children but to projects that would supposedly benefit them.

Nowadays, if people want to offer a similar gift, they can go to any number of crowdfunding sites where lots of small donors give money to a project or venture — like Fundly.com, Indiegogo.com, CrowdRise.com or GoFundMe.com — and bypass the middleman altogether.

On those sites, which usually make their money by taking a percentage of the funds raised, people with sympathetic stories seek sponsors — a young girl who needs a stem-cell treatment, a woman who wants money to adopt a child or a classroom of low-income students who want to visit Washington.

But crowdfunding raises questions. If young people give to these single-issue causes, is there less likelihood they will donate to the legacy charities such as the Red Cross, United Way and, yes, Save the Children? Does the individual and direct nature of crowdfunding act as a spur or a drain to such longtime nonprofits?

"Crowdfunding is particularly attractive to younger donors who are looking for a more direct connection to the causes and people they're supporting," said Katherina M. Rosqueta, executive director of the Center for High Impact Philanthropy at the University of Pennsylvania. "I think of it as a tool, one which might bring stories and issues to particular donors who wouldn't otherwise be aware and prompt them to give."

But a direct connection doesn't necessarily mean it is more effective. Ms. Rosqueta says the bigger, more established charities play a role that crowdfunding does not. These organizations "bring deep experience and knowledge to their area," she said. "They've had to measure and manage their own results for donors. People might feel a more direct connection in crowdfunding, but it doesn't mean it's doing the most good."

The money raised in crowdfunding — about $1.6 billion nationally and $2.7 billion worldwide in 2012, according to the research company Massolution — is minuscule compared with the approximately $300 billion raised by nonprofits in this country alone, according to Giving USA, the annual report of charitable donations.

But the nonprofits' figure isn't growing. Since the 1970s, charitable donations have made up about 2 percent of the gross domestic product and Americans, on average, give 2 percent of their gross income to charities — including universities and religious institutions. That comes to about $1,500 a year per household.

Donation and reward-based crowdfunding, which is growing off a decidedly lower base, increased by more than 85 percent worldwide in 2012 over the previous year, according to Massolution.

Christin Putnam of Larchmont, N.Y., discovered crowdfunding when someone she knew asked for support for a project, which is typical of many crowdfunding donors. "I give to projects that appeal to me on a personal level," said Ms. Putnam. Her donations, she said, "reflect my own quirky interests. For example, I have funded history books and maps for a classroom, organic seeds for a school classroom, a film about bullying and Jewish community project in the town of Auschwitz."

Ms. Putnam said that she still supported traditional philanthropies "because I agree with their mission and have longstanding ties," but said that giving to sites like donorchoose.org, which is for teachers, is more fun "and more like an impulse buy."

Research shows that impulse donating is common on crowdfunding sites, said Gregory Saxton, director of the Graduate Studies at the

Department of Communication at the State University of New York, Buffalo. But, he said, research also shows that many donors don't seem to particularly care whether or not a project they support is financially effective. Rather, they are swayed by attention-getting videos and sentimental stories rather than the depth of the need.

Charities have long used heart-rending photos, tear-jerking songs or poignant tales to attract donors. In an early version of crowdfunding, the newspaper magnate Joseph Pulitzer said in 1885 that he would print the name of every person who donated to the construction of a pedestal for the Statue of Liberty on the front page of his newspaper and would also print human interest stories sent along with the donations. Soon, more than 120,000 people had donated $100,000 — $2.3 million in current dollars — enough to pay for the pedestal.

Mr. Pulitzer may not have realized that he was combining the very ingredients that Danae Ringelmann, co-founder of Indiegogo.com, says inspires people to donate to crowdfunding: passion for the project, trust in the person behind it, involvement in something bigger than oneself and the receipt of a perk.

The traditional charities have not ignored the potential of crowdfunding. Ettore Rossetti, director of digital marketing and social media for Save the Children, said his organization had benefited from several crowdfunding appeals, and had also started some of its own campaigns. "The way charities used to be run was on brand loyalty," he said. "That's not so true anymore. There's a risk, if you're not nimble and don't participate in new media, you can absolutely be left behind."

But Mr. Rossetti also expressed concern that some people believed crowdfunding causes were better because they appeared to more directly help those in need. "I think crowdfunding is good, but there is the risk of being beholden to the whim of popularity," he said.

Others are worried about the tendency of crowdfunding to dismiss overhead and administrative costs as needless bureaucracy, without realizing the complicated causes that large charities address.

"A very simplistic project can be great, but if it becomes the sole means people give, we're going to end up addressing a much narrower set of social problems," said Ken Berger, president of Charity Navigator, which monitors nonprofits. "Take homelessness. It's not a simple story. We can't only focus on one aspect like job training or affordable housing."

Ms. Ringelmann of Indiegogo doesn't see a conflict. She says sites like hers can work with and help push traditional charities to be more transparent in how their money is spent.

The question will be if, like Ms. Putnam, most donors are willing to give to both traditional charities and crowdfunding. "We need traditional charities such as museums and universities because they are essential to our society," she said, "but we also need to support people outside the mainstream."

Kickstarter Focuses Its Mission on Altruism Over Profit

BY MIKE ISAAC AND DAVID GELLES | SEPT. 20, 2015

MANY TECHNOLOGY START-UPS aim to become "unicorns," the companies that get valued at $1 billion or more on their way to probable vast riches. Yancey Strickler and Perry Chen have no interest in that.

As co-founders of Kickstarter, the popular online crowdfunding website that lets people raise money to help fund all manner of projects, including cooking gadgets and movies, Mr. Strickler and Mr. Chen could have tried to take their company public or sell it, earning millions of dollars for themselves and other shareholders.

Instead, they announced on Sunday that Kickstarter was reincorporating as a "public benefit corporation," a legal change they said would ensure that money — or the promise of it — would not corrupt their company's mission of enabling creative projects to be funded.

"We don't ever want to sell or go public," said Mr. Strickler, Kickstarter's chief executive. "That would push the company to make choices that we don't think are in the best interest of the company."

Public benefit corporations are a relatively new designation that has been signed into law by a number of states. Delaware, where Kickstarter is reincorporating, began allowing public benefit corporations in 2013.

Under the designation, companies must aim to do something that would aid the public (such as Kickstarter's mission to "help bring creative projects to life") and include that goal in their corporate charter. Board members must also take that public benefit into account when making decisions, and the company has to report on its social impact.

"Public benefit corporations will harness the power of private enterprise to create public benefit," Gov. Jack Markell of Delaware said in 2013, adding that such companies "consider profit to be the means — not the exclusive end goal — of their business."

Kickstarter's move builds upon its decision last year to become a B Corporation, a voluntary designation certified by a nonprofit group called B Lab. To become a B Corp, companies must meet rigorous environmental and social-responsibility standards, which they report annually to shareholders — though taking on the status has no legal impact. Other companies, including the e-commerce site Etsy, which went public in April, and Warby Parker, the eyeglasses retailer, have also opted to become B Corps.

All of this stands in stark contrast to the behavior of many tech start-ups these days. With money having flowed freely into tech enterprises in recent years, businesses like the ride-hailing company Uber, the room-rental start-up Airbnb and the online storage service Dropbox have all raised billions from venture capitalists and big money managers, with the aim of large profits.

Becoming a public benefit corporation does not prevent Kickstarter from selling itself or going public, and it remains a for-profit entity. Still, as a B Corp and now a public benefit corporation, legal experts say, Kickstarter is holding itself to a particularly high standard of transparency.

"A public benefit corporation is only required to report its social and environmental performance to shareholders every two years," said Kyle Westaway, a lawyer based in New York and managing partner of his own practice, who works with public benefit corporations. "But Kickstarter chose to go above and beyond and report to the public every year as a B Corp. This represents a real commitment to transparency."

Kickstarter, which is based in New York, was founded by Mr. Chen, Mr. Strickler and Charles Adler, who is now an adviser, in 2009. Its site lets anyone pitch projects to the public to raise money, and Kickstarter earns fees from every successfully funded project on its platform. Kickstarter has helped fund high-profile products like the "Veronica Mars" movie and the Pebble smartwatch, but has also faced controversies, including complaints that prominent musicians and filmmakers have exploited the crowdfunding model while not being fully transparent with their backers.

For other companies, some of the stipulations Kickstarter put into its charter as a public benefit corporation would be anathema. Kickstarter is exceptionally charitable, for instance, donating 5 percent of after-tax profits to causes that support the arts and combat inequality. Kickstarter has also agreed to "not use loopholes or other esoteric but legal tax management strategies to reduce its tax burden."

Kickstarter decided to become a public benefit corporation because "there's a huge difference between a values document and the legal foundation of your company," said Mr. Chen, who serves as chairman but focuses on making art.

Kickstarter still has investors to answer to. While the company has not yet raised much money — less than $15 million, with the founders retaining majority ownership — some well-known tech investors have backed it. They include Chris Sacca, a former Google executive who became a big investor in Twitter, as well as Union Square Ventures, a venture capital firm based in New York, and Jack Dorsey, co-founder of Twitter and Square.

Some of the investors said they knew what they were getting into, as Mr. Chen and Mr. Strickler made it clear early on that they were not looking for a massive payday from Kickstarter. Mr. Sacca said he believed there were other ways for shareholders to see returns from their investment in Kickstarter besides an acquisition or an initial public offering. It helps that Kickstarter's financial trajectory has been strong. Mr. Chen and Mr. Strickler say their company has been profitable for years — in the $5 million to $10 million range per year for each of the last three years — and has continually reinvested that money in the business.

"It is a fast-growing, highly profitable enterprise. So, as an owner of the stock, I feel comfortable that I will be rewarded for that," Mr. Sacca said. "When the time is right, I'm confident that Kickstarter will return cash to their loyal shareholders."

Rejecting the idea of an I.P.O. or acquisition may hurt Kickstarter's recruiting, since those common practices attract engineers to start-ups with the promise of prosperity. But the Kickstarter co-founders said the company's stance had attracted like-minded people — those more focused on the overall mission and less on the value of their equity.

"It's allowed us to find people who have a similar idealism," Mr. Chen said.

Kickstarter has also taken the unconventional step of letting employees exercise their option grants for up to 10 years, even if they leave the company. And the co-founders said they planned to begin paying a dividend to shareholders and employees in the next few years.

"It's not going to be a huge lottery ticket," Mr. Chen said. "It's going to be profits shared on an annual basis. We'll all benefit from what's created."

Mr. Chen and Mr. Strickler said their ultimate hope was that becoming a public benefit corporation would set an example for the next generation of entrepreneurs.

"As younger companies come up and think about how they operate and how they want to be structured, maybe they won't be so easily swept up by all the usual choices," Mr. Chen said. "Maybe they'll be thinking long term, thinking about how to look after the things they care about."

GoFundMe Gone Wild

BY JUDITH NEWMAN | NOV. 6, 2015

AS SOMEONE WITH the keen observational skills of Mr. Magoo, it took me a long time to notice a problem social-media acquaintances had been talking about for months.

"I woke up to four new people today asking me for money on four different donation platforms," one friend said. "One was my ex-babysitter announcing her wedding and where I could send cash. No invitation to the wedding. Just cash."

"I'm a believer in giving to real charities: medical research, school drives, the Red Cross, et cetera," said Heidi Knodle, owner of a picture framing store in San Francisco. "I'm tired of people asking for a vacation, funds for a wedding or their college tuition."

The crime writer Mark Ebner, whose mailboxes have been increasingly filled with monetary requests, has a theory about it all. "I think online begging has become the new economy."

I thought my friends were exaggerating. After all, a visit to GoFundMe or YouCaring yields site after site of worthy donation recipients. People whose homes were wiped out by natural disasters. People with diseases I'd never heard of, with no insurance and staggering medical expenses. Kids trying to pay for their parents' funerals. Parents with seriously ill children wanting a trip to Disney World, and sick animals owned by people who couldn't afford the vet bills.

One man had set up a fund for a friend who needed to take a couple of months off while his wife died of brain cancer.

But then, there were others. Many, many others. Education funds are great, but do I really want to pay for a friend to travel to Peru to become a shaman?

Should the woman who has lost a lot of weight (good for you!) ask her friends to pay for $2,500 worth of laser skin tightening? What about the girl seeking $600 for her "personal development journey"?

ANDY RASH

(Not much to ask, but she was so beautiful, I didn't understand why she didn't develop herself into a model and make a whole lot more than that.)

Another woman was asking for help with the legal bills for her divorce, as her new husband had bolted to Israel. She was a little dramatic in her plea: "My life — the innocent, carefree life which I had known, and the blissful happy life of hopes and dreams shattered overnight. Instead of partaking of gourmet meals and donning my kalla/bridal trousseau, chaos and turmoil, sprinkled with vicious gossip became my daily food and clothing."

The requests continued.

Sponsorship for a child's figure skating lessons from a mother who, according to the friend who got daily reminders to donate, just renovated her kitchen.

Money for a power generator for a guy in Brooklyn who holds parties for artists, writers and musicians in a shack in his backyard, who said he is doing a project on "the history of shacks."

A talented writer who was having a rough patch put up a "birthday plea" for $2,000 — no, make that $200,000. A guy who needs a new MacBook after someone spilled a drink on his. The woman who just asked for $20,000 for plastic surgery because she had children early and "struggles with body image issues."

Or take the recent page of Larry Paciotti, a.k.a. the famous pornographic film director/drag queen Chi Chi LaRue, who was asking for $40,000 to extend his stay in rehab at Betty Ford. One non-funder on his funding page called the request "a gross abuse of fame ... Larry has plenty of personal resources available to secure this funding on his own."

And that, of course, is at the heart of the backlash: the sneaking suspicion that someone of considerable (or at least ample) means and/or connections is asking for help.

When Jane Green, the best-selling novelist, decided to go all Martha Stewart and put out a sumptuously designed cookbook called "Good Taste: Good Food. A Good Life — Collector's Edition," she asked friends and readers to send her $25 each on Kickstarter. The donation process included frequent updates and contests: Have lunch with Jane! Win a vintage Pyrex set! (I'm not quite sure what vintage Pyrex is, but apparently it exists.)

Many on her mailing list were taken aback; after all, this was a woman whose Instagram feed is pure real estate porn, who was the subject of a Financial Times article last year called "Jane Green: Chick-Lit Author and Property Tycoon" and who is married to one of the scions of the Warburg banking family.

Or as one friend who forwarded me her site put it, "I just got this from a multimillionaire."

"This is not a rich lady asking her readers to give her money for a vanity project," said Christy Fletcher, Ms. Green's agent. (Ms. Green declined to speak.)

"She started because she is very creative and she wanted creative control," Ms. Fletcher said. "It's like, if you want it, order it; if you don't, don't. It's just asking people to buy your work, only on Kickstarter instead of in a store."

Well, not quite.

Given the frequency of the email solicitations, and the level of intimacy expected in the exchanges (another would-be author offered "immortality" to one lucky donor by writing her into her novel for

$1,000), it's not quite like ordering on Amazon. It's more like Amazon stops by your house for a drink and at midnight is still chatting, while you try not to glance at your watch.

I wanted to find a sociologist to comment on this phenomenon. When I searched for "sociologist" and "GoFundMe," I came across this: "Send a sociologist to GDC!" Apparently a gamer working toward her Ph.D. in sociology needed money to attend a conference to complete her work on gender performance in rock music video games. That wasn't what I was looking for.

Ethan Mollick, however, was. He is an assistant professor of management at Wharton Business School who has studied online crowdfunding on sites like Indiegogo and Kickstarter. Professor Mollick explained that if I was looking at crowdfunding only as a means of raising money, I was missing the point.

"One of the surprises of reward-based crowdfunding is that money is only one piece of this," he said. "People use platforms like Kickstarter and Indiegogo not just to raise money for a project, but to gauge whether there's an audience, to build a community — and to get attention. No one has really studied the personal donation sites, but I suspect the exact same thing holds true there."

Indeed, Professor Mollick argues, personal sites may be even more about getting attention than getting money. A quick survey of sites shows that many people seem as interested in being the next guest on Ellen DeGeneres as in getting funds. (Meeting Ellen DeGeneres is a surprisingly common request on GoFundMe.)

Here's the question I can't stop asking myself: Has social media made our craving for attention and validation overwhelm all other considerations? There is nothing new about asking your friends for help (remember rent parties?), but that help was confined to a small group of people you actually knew.

Now, no such boundaries exist. Your 4,000 Facebook friends should know if you can't pay your rent — or your plastic surgery bill. And who knows? They may just pay up.

There was a time when there were needs, and there were wants, and we knew the difference. Now?

Now I'm not so sure.

JUDITH NEWMAN is working on a book based on her New York Times article "To Siri, With Love."

$400,000 Poured In for a Homeless Man, and Now He Wants It

BY SANDRA E. GARCIA | AUG. 29, 2018

WHEN A HOMELESS MAN in Philadelphia gave a stranded couple his last $20 so they could buy gas, they were so inspired that they started an online fund-raiser to help him.

The goal on GoFundMe was set at $10,000. But over nine months, more than 14,000 people donated over $400,000 to the man, Johnny Bobbitt Jr. Less inspiring: He says he has yet to see any of the money. He is still homeless and was panhandling until he checked into rehab. And he filed a lawsuit this week against the New Jersey couple, Mark D'Amico and Kate McClure.

"He is living off the kindness of strangers," Jacqueline Promislo, a lawyer for Mr. Bobbitt, said in an interview.

On Thursday, a New Jersey judge ordered the couple to transfer the money into an escrow account by Friday afternoon, The Philadelphia Inquirer reported.

The couple told their side of the story Monday morning on "Megyn Kelly Today" on NBC.

At first, Mr. D'Amico and Ms. McClure said, they tried to move the money to a bank account for Mr. Bobbitt, but he did not have any identification. They said that they gave him $25,000 in cash last Christmas but that Mr. Bobbitt spent all the money in 13 days. They added that Mr. Bobbitt had used their Lyft account to order a car service to take him to locations known for selling and buying drugs.

They decided to hold on to the rest for his own good, they said. "We didn't want to give him the whole $400,000," Mr. D'Amico said.

Instead of giving him more cash, they said, they tried to buy things for him. They helped him buy a trailer that he parked at their house.

"We took him and he picked it out," Mr. D'Amico said in the TV interview.

While that story played well on the show, Ms. Promislo, who said she was representing Mr. Bobbitt at no charge, said he had no trailer.

"They bought it in their name and kept it in their name," she said. "I believe they sold it."

As reported by The Inquirer last week, Mr. Bobbitt believed that the couple had been spending the money on vacations and a new BMW. The couple, who did not immediately respond to phone messages left on Wednesday, told "Megyn Kelly Today" the car they bought was used.

Ms. Promislo declined to say who was paying for Mr. Bobbitt's rehab, and how long he had been in drug treatment.

The judge's ruling on Thursday stipulated that the money will be controlled by Ms. Promislo's law firm, Cozen O'Connor, until the court determines how it will be managed, The Inquirer reported. The judge did not appoint a guardian for the account, but one could be appointed later.

A day before the ruling, Ms. Promislo said that Mr. Bobbitt "wants the money put in a trust and assistance figuring out how to spend it." She declined to say if a family member or her firm would be willing to take on that role.

"The money was never given for Mark or for Kate, but they put the money in their own personal account," she said.

Mr. D'Amico said in the TV interview, "I wanted to make sure that at the end of the day when he was ready, that there was something left for him."

He did admit to gambling $500 with Mr. Bobbitt's permission, but said that he had since repaid it.

Financial mismanagement of donations and fraud are not new problems for online crowdfunding sites.

"It happens more often than GoFundMe admits to," said Adrienne Gonzalez, who runs GoFraudMe.com, a watchdog site.

For example, she said, there have been many cases of people raising money for cancer that they do not have, or failing to turn over donations raised for expenses like funerals.

GoFundMe will refund donations to donors if it suspects misuse or make sure the money gets to the beneficiary, a spokesman said.

As for Mr. Bobbitt, Ms. Promislo said: "He wants a home. He wants his money."

GoFundMe Campaign to Build Border Wall Raises Millions, Riles Migrant Advocates

BY DAN LEVIN | DEC. 21, 2018

CROWDFUNDING DONATIONS HAVE paid for medical and legal bills, wildfire losses and college tuition. Now, a GoFundMe campaign aims to finance one the most hotly debated issues in American politics: President Trump's long-promised border wall.

The campaign, called "We The People Will Fund The Wall" and launched this week by a disabled Florida veteran, had raised more than $13 million from more than 213,000 people by Friday afternoon. The goal? $1 billion.

"Americans are putting their money where their mouth is," the campaign's founder, Brian Kolfage, said in an interview Friday. "They're willing to put money down to show politicians this is what they want."

Mr. Kolfage — a triple amputee who served in Iraq and who ran a right-wing website that was eventually removed by Facebook — is hoping to raise even greater sums to cover construction of a barrier between the United States and Mexico. He suggested on the GoFundMe page that if the 63 million people who voted for Mr. Trump were to each donate $80, they would raise more than $5 billion, the amount Mr. Trump is seeking for the wall.

"As a veteran who has given so much, 3 limbs, I feel deeply invested to this nation to ensure future generations have everything we have today," Mr. Kolfage, 37, wrote in the fund-raiser description. "Too many Americans have been murdered by illegal aliens and too many illegals are taking advantage of the United States taxpayers with no means of ever contributing to our society."

Mr. Kolfage, a Purple Heart recipient who lives in Miramar Beach, Fla., wrote on the GoFundMe page that he began the drive out of frustration that Mr. Trump's signature campaign promise remained unfulfilled. "It's time we uphold our laws, and get this wall BUILT!," he wrote. "It's up to Americans to help out and pitch in to get this project rolling."

In a phone interview, Mr. Kolfage said the public outpouring of donations only underscored the exasperation felt by those who supported the wall project. "Americans are frustrated with the way things are going and politicians holding us all hostage," he said.

The campaign went viral as Mr. Trump appeared to back down from his threat to shut down the government unless Congress allocated $5 billion for the wall, a capitulation that outraged his most ardent supporters and right-wing media pundits alike. The president later said on Twitter that Mexico would indirectly pay for the wall through a new North American free trade deal. But on Thursday, Mr. Trump told House Republican leaders he would not sign a stopgap spending bill to avert a shutdown if it did not include border-wall funding. The House on Thursday evening passed stopgap spending legislation with an additional $5.7 billion for wall construction, but it is expected to fail in the Senate, where Democratic votes are needed to top the 60-vote threshold.

Like Mr. Trump, Mr. Kolfage has focused his wrath on congressional Democrats, whom he blames for refusing to fund the project. "They'd rather see President Trump fail, than see America succeed," he wrote on the fund-raiser page.

Immigration advocacy groups condemned the GoFundMe campaign, calling it a misguided venture fueled by xenophobia.

"The fund-raiser is a direct consequence of the president's yearslong fearmongering about immigrants," said Jonathan Ryan, executive director of the Refugee and Immigrant Center for Education and Legal Services, a Texas nonprofit known as Raices. This summer, a Facebook fund-raising campaign for the group raked in more than $20 million from more than 525,000 people, the largest single fund-raiser in the social media platform's history.

Dismayed by Mr. Kolfage's efforts, a number of people started online campaigns for Raices in recent days, including one created Thursday that had raised nearly $100,000 by late Friday afternoon. "We're not scared of those who would support President Trump's racist border wall. We know it will go down as a historical blunder and, if built, a scar across our country," Mr. Ryan said in an email.

Mr. Kolfage dismissed the criticism, saying he simply opposes illegal immigration. "Just go through the front door," he said. "Bring all these migrants in, verify them, vet them. I'm all for it."

Mr. Kolfage assured donors that "100% of your donations will go to the Trump Wall," and that his team had contacted the Trump administration about securing the funds. He also wrote that he was working with a law firm to draft a contract that would "bind the government to using the funds for the border wall itself, nothing else."

To allay any doubts, Mr. Kolfage's campaign page cited the 2012 Washington Monument restoration project, which repaired earthquake damage to the 555-foot obelisk with $7.5 million allocated by the government and a matching donation made by a billionaire to the Trust for the National Mall, a nonprofit public-private partnership with the National Park Service. If the crowdfunding project fails to reach its goal, Mr. Kolfage promised to refund every donation. "This won't be easy, but it's our duty as citizens," he wrote.

But it is not that simple. The Department of Homeland Security would not be able to accept the donations without congressional approval.

"Congress would still have to enact a statute permitting this," said David Bier, a policy analyst at the libertarian Cato Institute. "But current law prohibits the administration from taking this money and spending it, and it also violates the law to accept donations that bind the hands of the administration."

Mr. Kolfage said in the interview that he had spoken to someone in the White House, but declined to identify the person. "I think it's gone all the way up to President Trump," he said. He added that Representative Jim Jordan, Republican of Ohio, had called him to say that the GoFundMe campaign had impacted Thursday's vote.

Since Mr. Kolfage started his campaign, numerous copycats have started their own wall crowdfunding efforts. Some have raised a few thousand dollars, but most remain at $0. It is not the first time conservatives have turned to the internet for help in paying for a physical barrier. In 2011, Arizona lawmakers started an online fund for a border fence, which was never built.

The campaign's viral success may stem in part from Mr. Kolfage's national profile as a conservative political activist who ran a political website that was removed by Facebook in October, an action that drew the attention of Fox News.

According to his website, which describes him as "the most severely wounded US Airman to survive his wounds," Mr. Kolfage was on his second deployment to Iraq in September 2004, when a 107mm enemy rocket shell exploded three feet away from him. One of his lungs collapsed and three of his limbs were mangled, but medics saved his life. Despite amputations of both legs and his right hand, Mr. Kolfage completed rehabilitation at Walter Reed Medical Center in Washington in just 11 months, and he later became a motivational speaker.

In October, Facebook removed hundreds of political pages for "coordinated inauthentic behavior," including Mr. Kolfage's Right Wing News, he told Fox News that month. He denied claims made by NBC News on Thursday that he ran a series of affiliate websites that promoted false political conspiracy theories and racist content. In the wake of the purge, Mr. Kolfage launched a website that accuses Facebook of censoring conservative views, but his GoFundMe page makes no mention of these websites.

GoFundMe to Refund Border Wall Donations After Fund-Raiser Falls Short

BY MIHIR ZAVERI | JAN. 11, 2019

THE CROWDFUNDING PLATFORM GoFundMe said that more than $20 million in donations were slated to be refunded after a campaign to raise $1 billion for the Trump administration to build a wall on the border with Mexico had fallen well short of its goal.

The fund-raising campaign, which began last month, had gone viral as President Trump's attempt to get Congress to pay for the wall fueled a heated political dispute and resulted in a partial shutdown of the federal government.

More than 325,000 donors had pledged in the GoFundMe campaign that the organizer, a veteran from Florida named Brian Kolfage, said would have been used for President Trump's border wall.

But in a note posted on the campaign's website on Friday, Mr. Kolfage said the federal government would not be able to accept the donations "anytime soon."

Mr. Kolfage said in an interview that donating to the government would have required approval from Congress and that he knew that a Democrat-controlled House would not give its approval.

Instead, Mr. Kolfage said, he has formed a Florida-based nonprofit organization called We Build the Wall that will use donations to finance a private effort to build parts of the wall where private landowners allow construction.

GoFundMe donors would have to proactively choose to redirect their money to the nonprofit; otherwise, they would be refunded.

Mr. Kolfage said he did not know exactly how many donors would want to redirect their money nor how many landowners would want parts of the wall constructed on their properties.

“When Americans see us completing real miles of beautiful wall, we know that we will raise the many billions we need to finally secure the entire border,” Mr. Kolfage said on the updated GoFundMe campaign page.

The Department of Homeland Security and the Trump administration did not respond to requests for comment on Friday evening on the possibility of a privately funded effort to build the wall.

Typically, GoFundMe campaigns can still collect money even if they do not meet their goal.

But Bobby Whithorne, a spokesman for GoFundMe, said in a statement on Friday that Mr. Kolfage’s original campaign page had said “If we don’t reach our goal or come significantly close we will refund every single penny” and that “100% of your donations will go to the Trump Wall. If for ANY reason we don’t reach our goal we will refund your donation.”

Mr. Whithorne said that since the campaign was not going to reach the $1 billion goal, and that both GoFundMe and Mr. Kolfage had determined the money raised could not be given to the federal government, GoFundMe had contacted all donors to the original campaign about the refund.

Donors can ask for a refund immediately, Mr. Whithorne said, but if they do not choose to redirect their money to the nonprofit, they will automatically receive a refund in 90 days.

Immigration advocacy groups had condemned the GoFundMe campaign as a xenophobic result of fearmongering about immigrants. Some had started competing fund-raising campaigns to raise money for Refugee and Immigrant Center for Education and Legal Services, a Texas nonprofit known as Raices.

Jonathan Ryan, president and chief executive of Raices, said that despite the change in Mr. Kolfage’s campaign, the original critiques of it still stand.

“It’s a difference without a change,” Mr. Ryan said. “The wall remains the wrong direction for us as a country, something that will not help advance any of our national interests and that would only serve to further harm vulnerable refugees and immigrants seeking protection in our country."

This week, Mr. Trump appeared on television in an attempt to pressure Congress into paying for the border wall, characterizing the situation at the Mexican border as a "humanitarian crisis" that was exposing the country to crime, drugs and terrorism.

Experts, however, point out that migrant border crossings have been declining over about two decades. The State Department said in a recent report that there was "no credible evidence" that terrorist groups had sent operatives to enter the country through Mexico.

Everything Is for Sale Now. Even Us.

OPINION | BY RUTH WHIPPMAN | NOV. 24, 2018

The constant pressure to sell ourselves on every possible platform has produced its own brand of modern anxiety.

THERE IS SOMETHING about the consumer madness of the holiday season that makes me think of my friend Rebecca's mother. When I was in middle school, she had a side hustle selling acrylic-rhinestone bug brooches. The jewelry was hard to move on its merits — even for the 1980s it was staggeringly ugly. But what she lacked in salable product, she made up for in sheer selling stamina. Every sleepover, school fair or birthday party, out would come the tray of bejeweled grasshoppers and stag beetles, glinting with Reagan-era menace.

Presumably someone was making money from this venture — some proto-Trump barking orders from his tax haven — but it certainly didn't seem to be Rebecca's mother, whose sales pitches took on an ever more shrill note of desperation.

Soon she had given up even the basic social pretense that we might actually want the brooches. The laws of supply and demand morphed seamlessly into the laws of guilt and obligation, and then into the laws of outright malice, mirroring the trajectory of capitalism itself.

At that time, when naked hawking to your friends was still considered an etiquette blunder, the sales pitches by Rebecca's mother felt embarrassing — as gaudy and threatening to the social ecosystem as a purple rhinestone daddy longlegs. But 30 years later, at the height of the gig economy, when the foundation of working life has apparently become selling your friends things they don't want, I look back to that raw need in Rebecca's mother's eyes with something terrifyingly approaching recognition.

As a writer, I am part of the 35 percent of the American work force that now works freelance in some capacity, either as a main source of

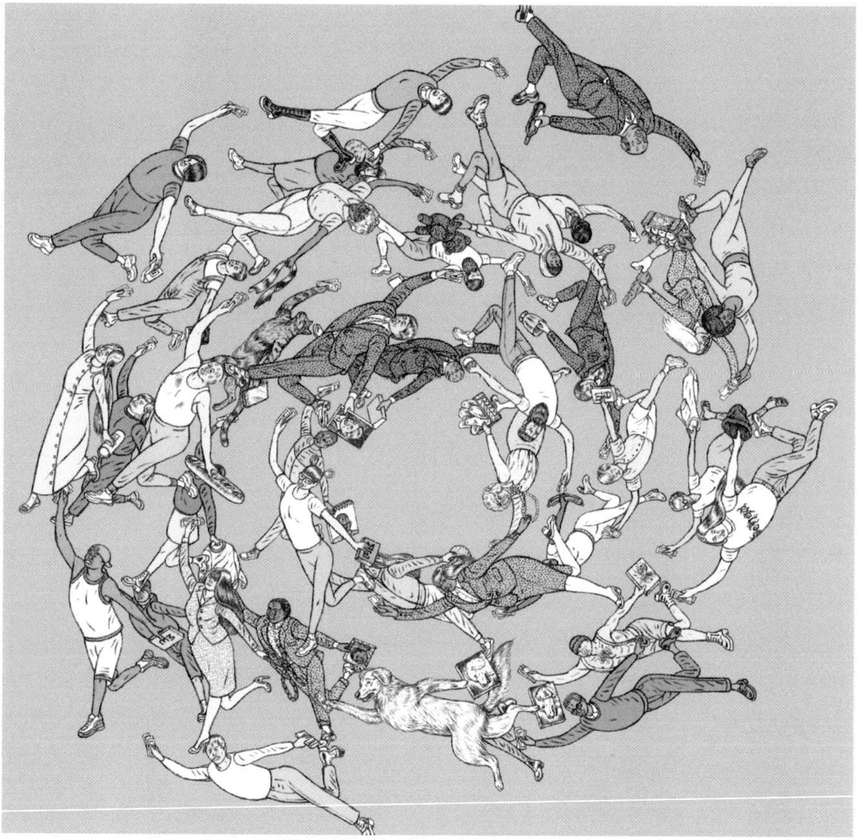

TIM ENTHOVEN

income or as some kind of side hustle. This number is growing constantly — 94 percent of the new jobs created in the last decade or so were freelance or contract-based.

When we think “gig economy,” we tend to picture an Uber driver or a TaskRabbit tasker rather than a lawyer or a doctor, but in reality, this scrappy economic model — grubbing around for work, all big dreams and bad health insurance — will soon catch up with the bulk of America’s middle class.

Major companies now outsource many of even their most skilled jobs, ditching their in-house lawyers and I.T. support teams in favor of on-demand contractors, paid by the hour. More than 18 million Americans are now involved in some kind of direct sales or multilevel marketing scheme, shelling out hundreds of dollars on vitamins or juicers or leggings, then frantically attempting to recoup the money by flogging them to friends and neighbors. Economists predict that by 2027, gig workers of varying descriptions will make up more than half of the work force. An estimated 47 percent of millennials already work in this way.

It certainly feels familiar. Almost everyone I know now has some kind of hustle, whether job, hobby, or side or vanity project. Share my blog post, buy my book, click on my link, follow me on Instagram, visit my Etsy shop, donate to my Kickstarter, crowdfund my heart surgery. It's as though we are all working in Walmart on an endless Black Friday of the soul.

Being sold to can be socially awkward, for sure, but when it comes to corrosive self-doubt, being the seller is a thousand times worse. The constant curation of a salable self demanded by the new economy can be a special hellspring of anxiety.

Like many modern workers, I find that only a small percentage of my job is now actually doing my job. The rest is performing a million acts of unpaid micro-labor that can easily add up to a full-time job in itself. Tweeting and sharing and schmoozing and blogging. Liking and commenting on others' tweets and shares and schmoozes and blogs. Ambivalently "maintaining a presence on social media," attempting to sell a semi-fictional, much more appealing version of myself in the vain hope that this might somehow help me sell some actual stuff at some unspecified future time.

The trick of doing this well, of course, is to act as if you aren't doing it at all — as if this is simply how you like to unwind in the evening, by sharing your views on pasta sauce with your 567,000 followers. Seeing the slick charm of successful online "influencers" spurs me to download e-courses on how to "crack Instagram" or "develop my personal brand story." But as soon as I hand over my credit card details, I am flooded with vague self-disgust. I instantly abandon the courses and revert to my usual business model — badgering and guilting my friends across a range of online platforms, employing the personal brand story of "pleeeeeeeeeeaassssee."

As my friend Helena (Buy her young adult novel! Available on Amazon!) puts it, buying, promoting or sharing your friend's "thing" is now a tax payable for modern friendship. But this expectation becomes its own monster. I find myself auditing my friends' loyalty based on their efforts. Who bought it? Who shared it on Facebook? Was it a share from the heart, or a "duty share" — with that telltale, torturous phrasing that squeaks past the minimum social requirement but deftly dissociates the sharer from the product: "My friend wrote a book — I haven't read it, but maybe you should."

In this cutthroat human marketplace, we are worth only as much as the sum of our metrics, so checking those metrics can become obsessive. What's my Amazon ranking? How many likes? How many retweets? How many followers? (The word "followers" is in itself a clear indicator of something psychologically unhealthy going on — the standard term for the people we now spend the bulk of our time with sounds less like a functioning human relationship than the P.R. materials of the Branch Davidians.)

Of course a fair chunk of this mass selling frenzy is motivated by money. With a collapsing middle class, as well as close to zero job security and none of the benefits associated with it, self-marketing has become, for many, a necessity in order to eat.

But what's more peculiar is just how imperfectly all this correlates with financial need or even greed. The sad truth is that many of us would probably make more money stacking shelves or working at the drive-through than selling our "thing." The real prize is deeper, more existential. What this is really about, for many of us, is a roaring black hole of psychological need.

After a couple of decades of constant advice to "follow our passions" and "live our dreams," for a certain type of relatively privileged modern freelancer, nothing less than total self-actualization at work now seems enough. But this leaves us with an angsty mismatch between personal expectation and economic reality. So we shackle our self-worth to the success of these projects — the book or blog post or range of crocheted stuffed penguins becomes a proxy for our very soul. In the new economy you can be your own boss and your own ugly bug brooch.

Kudos to whichever neoliberal masterminds came up with this system. They sell this infinitely seductive torture to us as "flexible working" or "being the C.E.O. of You!" and we jump at it, salivating, because on its best days, the freelance life really can be all of that.

But as long as we are happy to be paid for our labor in psychological rather than financial rewards, those at the top are delighted to comply. While we grub and scrabble and claw at one another chasing these tiny pellets of self-esteem, the bug-brooch barons still pocket the actual cash.

This is the future, and research suggests that it's a rat race that is already taking a severe toll on our psyches. A 2017 study suggests that this trend toward increasingly market-driven human interaction is making us paranoid, jittery, self-critical and judgmental.

Analyzing data from the Multidimensional Perfectionism Scale from 1989 to 2016, the study's authors found a surprisingly large increase over this period in three distinct types of perfectionism: "Self-orientated," whereby we hold ourselves to increasingly unrealistic standards and judge ourselves harshly when we fail to meet them; "socially prescribed," in which we are convinced that other people judge us harshly; and "other-orientated," in which we get our revenge by judging them just as harshly. These elements of perfectionism positively correlate with mental health problems, including anxiety, depression and even suicide, which are also on the rise.

The authors describe this new-normal mind-set as a "sense of self overwhelmed by pathological worry and a fear of negative social evaluation." Hmm. Maybe I should make that my personal brand story.

RUTH WHIPPMAN is the author of "America the Anxious: Why Our Search for Happiness Is Driving Us Crazy and How to Find It for Real."

Glossary

altruism Unselfish regard for the welfare of others.

beta-test A trial of machinery, software or other products, in the final stages of development.

campaign Organized work toward a certain goal.

community A feeling of fellowship with others, or an actual group of people, resulting from shared attitudes, goals or interests.

crowd A group of people who are linked by a common interest or activity.

crowdfunding The practice of funding a project or venture by raising many small amounts of money from a large community of people via the Internet.

crowdfunding platform A website that provides a way for people to give money in support of a person, project or entity.

donation Something offered to charity, especially a sum of money.

entrepreneur A person who organizes and operates a business or businesses, often taking on financial risk to do so.

equity The value of the shares issued by a company.

fund-raising The seeking of financial support for a particular cause.

grant A sum of money given by a government or other organization for a certain purpose.

investor A person or organization that puts money into businesses or property expecting to achieve a profit.

nonprofit organization A group organized for purposes other than generating profit, and in which no income from the organization is distributed to its members, directors or officers.

social media Websites and applications that enable users to create and share content or to participate in social networking.

solicit To ask for or to try to obtain something from someone.

sponsor An individual or organization that pays some or all of the costs involved in staging an event in return for advertising.

stakeholder A person with an interest or concern in something, especially a business.

start-up A company in the first stage of its operations, often initially bankrolled by its entrepreneurial founders as it develops a product or service for which it perceives a demand.

Media Literacy Terms

"Media literacy" refers to the ability to access, understand, critically assess and create media. The following terms are important components of media literacy, and they will help you critically engage with the articles in this title.

balance Principle of journalism that both perspectives of an argument should be presented in a fair way.

editorial Article of opinion or interpretation.

feature story Article designed to entertain as well as to inform.

human interest story A type of story that focuses on individuals and how events or issues affect their life, generally offering a sense of relatability to the reader.

impartiality Principle of journalism that a story should not reflect a journalist's bias and should contain balance.

intention The motive or reason behind something, such as the publication of a news story.

interview story A type of story in which the facts are gathered primarily by interviewing another person or persons.

motive The reason behind something, such as the publication of a news story or a source's perspective on an issue.

op-ed An opinion piece that reflects a prominent individual's opinion on a topic of interest.

tone A manner of expression in writing or speech.

Media Literacy Questions

1. Analyze the authors' reporting in "Young Scientists Embrace Crowdfunding" (on page 11) and "New Crowdfunding Rules Let the Small Fry Swim With Sharks" (on page 49). Do you think one journalist is more balanced in their reporting than the other? If so, why do you think so?

2. What type of story is "Crowdfunding Tips for Turning Inspiration Into Reality" (on page 19)? Can you identify another article in this collection that is the same type of story? What elements helped you come to your conclusion?

3. Compare the headlines of "Smell of the Greasepaint, the Funds of the Crowd" (on page 81) and "Kickstarter as a Path to Grammy Nominations, Far Beyond the Indie Scene" (on page 90). Which is a more compelling headline, and why? How could the less compelling headline be changed to better draw the reader's interest?

4. Does "Video Game Raised $148 Million From Fans. Now It's Raising Concerns." (on page 96) use multiple sources? What are the strengths of using multiple sources in a journalistic piece? What are the weaknesses of relying heavily on only one or a few sources?

5. Identify the various sources cited in the article "A Crowdfunding Campaign Tries to Save Greece" (on page 115). How does Katie Rogers attribute information to each of these sources in her article? How effective are her attributions in helping the reader identify her sources?

6. What is the intention of the article "Muslim Groups Raise Thousands for Pittsburgh Synagogue Shooting Victims" (on page 135)? How effectively does it achieve its intended purpose?

7. What type of story is "In Defense of the Personal Crowdfunding Campaign" (on page 148)? Can you identify another article in this collection that is the same type of story? What elements helped you come to your conclusion?

8. "At 12, He Lost His Best Friend. He Found a Way to Remember Him." (on page 171) is an example of a human interest story. What is the purpose of a human interest story? Do you feel this article achieved that purpose?

9. In "The Effect Crowdfunding Has on Venerable Nonprofits Raises Concern" (on page 184), Alina Tugend directly quotes several sources. What are the strengths of a direct quote as opposed to a paraphrase? What are the weaknesses?

10. "GoFundMe Gone Wild" (on page 192) features an illustration. What does this illustration add to the article?

11. Does Sandra E. Garcia demonstrate the journalistic principle of impartiality in her article "$400,000 Poured In for a Homeless Man, and Now He Wants It" (on page 197)? If so, how did she do so? If not, what could she have included to make her article more impartial?

12. The article "Everything Is for Sale Now. Even Us." (on page 207) is an example of an op-ed. Identify how Ruth Whippman's attitude and tone help convey her opinion on the topic.

Citations

All citations in this list are formatted according to the Modern Language Association's (MLA) style guide.

BOOK CITATION

THE NEW YORK TIMES EDITORIAL STAFF. *Crowdfunding*. New York: New York Times Educational Publishing, 2020.

ONLINE ARTICLE CITATIONS

ALDEN, WILLIAM. "Crowdfunding Site CircleUp Raises $14 Million." *The New York Times*, 26 Mar. 2014, https://dealbook.nytimes.com/2014/03/26/crowdfunding-site-circleup-raises-14-million/.

ASTOR, MAGGIE. "GoFundMe Campaign for Christine Blasey Ford Takes Off After Testimony." *The New York Times*, 27 Sept. 2018, https://www.nytimes.com/2018/09/27/us/politics/blasey-ford-gofundme-kavanaugh-.html.

BEARDMORE, MATT. "With Help From Kickstarter, Chicago Gets a Museum That Relishes the Hot Dog." *The New York Times*, 18 Sept. 2015, https://www.nytimes.com/2015/09/18/travel/chicago-foodseum-kickstarter.html.

BROMWICH, JONAH ENGEL. "Secret Hitler, a Game That Simulates Fascism's Rise, Becomes a Hit." *The New York Times*, 5 Sept. 2017, https://www.nytimes.com/2017/09/05/business/secret-hitler-game.html.

CORREAL, ANNIE. "Women Ask 'What if It Were Me?' and Rush to Aid Separated Families." *The New York Times*, 20 July 2018, https://www.nytimes.com/2018/07/20/nyregion/crowdfunding-immigrant-children-separated.html.

COWLEY, STACY. "Ever Wanted to Back a Start-Up? Indiegogo Opens the Door to Small Investors." *The New York Times*, 15 Nov. 2016, https://www.nytimes.com/2016/11/15/business/ever-wanted-to-back-a-start-up-indiegogo-opens-the-door-to-small-investors.html.

COWLEY, STACY. "Global Brands, Taking Cue From Tinkerers, Explore Crowdfunding." *The New York Times*, 6 Jan. 2016, https://www.nytimes

.com/2016/01/07/business/global-brands-taking-cue-from-tinkerers-explore-crowdfunding.html.

COWLEY, STACY. "New Crowdfunding Rules Let the Small Fry Swim With Sharks." *The New York Times*, 14 May 2016, https://www.nytimes.com/2016/05/15/business/dealbook/new-crowdfunding-rules-let-the-small-fry-swim-with-sharks.html.

COWLEY, STACY. "S.E.C. Gives Small Investors Access to Equity Crowdfunding." *The New York Times*, 30 Oct. 2015, https://www.nytimes.com/2015/10/31/business/dealbook/sec-gives-small-investors-access-to-equity-crowdfunding.html.

ELBEIN, ASHER. "Utah Paleontologists Turn to Crowdfunding for Raptor Project." *The New York Times*, 28 Aug. 2017, https://www.nytimes.com/2017/08/28/science/utah-paleontologists-turn-to-crowdfunding-for-raptor-project.html.

EMBER, SYDNEY. "Start-Ups Turn to the Crowd for Financing." *The New York Times*, 10 Dec. 2014, https://dealbook.nytimes.com/2014/12/10/start-ups-turn-to-the-crowd-for-financing/.

GARCIA, SANDRA E. "$400,000 Poured In for a Homeless Man, and Now He Wants It." *The New York Times*, 29 Aug. 2018, https://www.nytimes.com/2018/08/29/us/homeless-man-go-fund-me.html.

GUSTKE, CONSTANCE. "Managing Health Costs With Crowdfunding." *The New York Times*, 30 Jan. 2015, https://www.nytimes.com/2015/01/31/business/managing-health-costs-with-crowdfunding.html.

HAAG, MATTHEW. "Muslim Groups Raise Thousands for Pittsburgh Synagogue Shooting Victims." *The New York Times*, 29 Oct. 2018, https://www.nytimes.com/2018/10/29/us/muslims-raise-money-pittsburgh-synagogue.html.

HAIGNEY, SOPHIE. "Los Angeles Museum Starts a Kickstarter Campaign for a Traveling Egg-Shaped Gallery." *The New York Times*, 9 June 2017, https://www.nytimes.com/2017/06/09/arts/design/los-angeles-museum-starts-a-kickstarter-campaign-for-a-traveling-egg-shaped-gallery.html.

HAUSER, CHRISTINE. "Texas Lawmaker Proposes Crowdfunding to Tackle Backlog of Rape Kits." *The New York Times*, 15 Mar. 2017, https://www.nytimes.com/2017/03/15/us/rape-kits-texas-untested.html.

HEALY, PATRICK. "Smell of the Greasepaint, the Funds of the Crowd." *The New York Times*, 27 July 2014, https://www.nytimes.com/2014/07/28/theater/smell-of-the-greasepaint-the-funds-of-the-crowd.html.

HOLSON, LAURA M. "As Funeral Crowdfunding Grows, So Do the Risks." *The*

New York Times, 5 June 2018, https://www.nytimes.com/2018/06/05/business/funerals-crowdsourcing-crowdfunding-scams.html.

ISAAC, MIKE, AND DAVID GELLES. "Kickstarter Focuses Its Mission on Altruism Over Profit." *The New York Times*, 20 Sept. 2015, https://www.nytimes.com/2015/09/21/technology/kickstarters-altruistic-vision-profits-as-the-means-not-the-mission.html.

ITZKOFF, DAVE. " 'Veronica Mars' Fans Are Happy to Finance a Reunion." *The New York Times*, 5 Mar. 2014, https://www.nytimes.com/2014/03/09/movies/veronica-mars-fans-are-happy-to-finance-a-reunion.html.

KULISH, NICHOLAS, AND NATHANIEL POPPER. "Crowdfunding Helps Rescue Refugees Upended by Travel Ban." *The New York Times*, 9 Feb. 2017, https://www.nytimes.com/2017/02/09/us/travel-ban-crowdfunding.html.

LAPIDOS, JULIET. "Celebrities With Their Hands Out." *The New York Times*, 14 Sept. 2013, https://www.nytimes.com/2013/09/15/opinion/sunday/celebrities-with-their-hands-out.html.

LAPORTE, NICOLE. "Medical Care, Aided by the Crowd." *The New York Times*, 13 Apr. 2013, https://www.nytimes.com/2013/04/14/business/watsi-a-crowdfunding-site-offers-help-with-medical-care.html.

LEVIN, DAN. "GoFundMe Campaign to Build Border Wall Raises Millions, Riles Migrant Advocates." *The New York Times*, 21 Dec. 2018, https://www.nytimes.com/2018/12/21/us/gofundme-wall-border-border-mexico.html.

LEWIS-KRAUS, GIDEON. "ZPM Espresso and the Rage of the Jilted Crowd-funder." *The New York Times*, 30 Apr. 2015, https://www.nytimes.com/2015/05/03/magazine/zpm-espresso-and-the-rage-of-the-jilted-crowdfunder.html.

LIEBER, RON. "In Defense of the Personal Crowdfunding Campaign." *The New York Times*, 20 Nov. 2015, https://www.nytimes.com/2015/11/21/your-money/in-defense-of-the-personal-crowdfunding-campaign.html.

LONDOÑO, ERNESTO. "In Brazil, 'Queer Museum' Is Censored, Debated, Then Celebrated." *The New York Times*, 26 Aug. 2018, https://www.nytimes.com/2018/08/26/world/americas/queer-museum-rio-de-janeiro-brazil.html.

MARTIN, CLAIRE. "Taking Guns Off the Streets, $100 at a Time." *The New York Times*, 7 July 2017, https://www.nytimes.com/2017/07/07/business/taking-guns-off-the-streets-100-at-a-time.html.

MURPHY, KATE. "Crowdfunding Tips for Turning Inspiration Into Reality." *The New York Times*, 22 Jan. 2014, https://www.nytimes.com/2014/01/23/technology/personaltech/crowdfunding-tips-for-turning-inspiration-into-reality.html.

NEWMAN, JUDITH. "GoFundMe Gone Wild." *The New York Times*, 6 Nov. 2015, https://www.nytimes.com/2015/11/08/fashion/gofundme-gone-wild.html.

OLSON, ELIZABETH. "Soliciting Funds From the Crowd? Results Will Vary." *The New York Times*, 19 Mar. 2014, https://www.nytimes.com/2014/03/20/arts/artsspecial/soliciting-funds-from-the-crowd-results-will-vary.html.

PARKER, LAURA. "Video Game Raised $148 Million From Fans. Now It's Raising Concerns." *The New York Times*, 10 May 2017, https://www.nytimes.com/2017/05/10/technology/personaltech/video-game-raised-148-million-from-fans-now-its-raising-issues.html.

PIANIGIANI, GAIA. "Florence's Answer to Mafia Violence: A Painting's Loving Restoration." *The New York Times*, 25 May 2018, https://www.nytimes.com/2018/05/25/world/europe/uffizi-florence-mafia-card-player.html.

POPPER, NATHANIEL. "Doubts Arise as Investors Flock to Crowdfunded Start-Ups" *The New York Times*, 24 Jan. 2017, https://www.nytimes.com/2017/01/24/business/dealbook/crowdfunding-fraud-investing-startups.html.

RAO, TEJAL. "Crowdfunding a Well-Deserved Break." *The New York Times*, 25 Apr. 2017, https://www.nytimes.com/2017/04/25/insider/street-vendor-crowdfunding-a-well-deserved-break.html.

ROGERS, KATIE. "A Crowdfunding Campaign Tries to Save Greece." *The New York Times*, 30 June 2015, https://www.nytimes.com/2015/07/01/world/europe/a-crowdfunding-campaign-tries-to-save-greece.html.

ROGERS, KATIE. "How a Homeless Teenager's Viral Story Caused a Battle Over GoFundMe Money." *The New York Times*, 26 July 2016, https://www.nytimes.com/2016/07/27/us/how-a-homeless-teenagers-viral-story-caused-a-battle-over-gofundme-money.html.

SHEAR, MICHAEL D. "Obama Turns to Crowdfunding to Aid Fleeing Syrians." *The New York Times*, 6 Oct. 6 2015, https://www.nytimes.com/2015/10/07/world/middleeast/obama-turns-to-crowdfunding-to-aid-fleeing-syrians.html.

SISARIO, BEN. "Kickstarter as a Path to Grammy Nominations, Far Beyond the Indie Scene." *The New York Times*, 2 Feb. 2016, https://www.nytimes.com/2016/02/03/arts/music/kickstarter-as-a-path-to-grammy-nominations-far-beyond-the-indie-scene.html.

SISARIO, BEN. "Neil Young's Digital Music Project Raises $6.2 Million Online." *The New York Times*, 15 Apr. 2014, https://artsbeat.blogs.nytimes.com/2014/04/15/neil-youngs-digital-music-project-raises-6-2-million-online.

SLIVKA, KELLY. "Young Scientists Embrace Crowdfunding." *The New York*

Times, 29 May 2012, https://green.blogs.nytimes.com/2012/05/29/young-scientists-embrace-crowdfunding.

SMITH, RANDALL. "Crowdfunding a $500 Million Ferris Wheel, With a Wall Street Spin." *The New York Times*, 7 Sept. 2015, https://www.nytimes.com/2015/09/08/business/dealbook/crowdfunding-a-500-million-ferris-wheel-with-a-wall-street-spin.html.

STEVENS, MATT. "At 12, He Lost His Best Friend. He Found a Way to Remember Him." *The New York Times*, 12 Dec. 2018, https://www.nytimes.com/2018/12/12/us/michigan-boy-headstone.html.

TRUMP, ROB. "Why Would You Ever Give Money Through Kickstarter?" *The New York Times*, 8 Feb. 2013, https://www.nytimes.com/2013/02/10/magazine/why-would-you-ever-give-money-through-kickstarter.html.

TUGEND, ALINA. "The Effect Crowdfunding Has on Venerable Nonprofits Raises Concern." *The New York Times*, 7 Feb. 2014, https://www.nytimes.com/2014/02/08/your-money/crowdfundings-effect-on-venerable-nonprofits-raises-concern.html.

VICTOR, DANIEL. "His Wife Died in the Santa Fe School Shooting. The World's Sympathy May Keep Him Alive." *The New York Times*, 22 May 2018, https://www.nytimes.com/2018/05/22/us/gofundme-cancer-patient-santa-fe.html.

WALDSTEIN, DAVID. "Donations Will Help Former Tennis Prodigy Get Career-Saving Surgery." *The New York Times*, 23 Oct. 2017, https://www.nytimes.com/2017/10/23/sports/tennis/tornado-alicia-black-surgery.html.

WHIPPMAN, RUTH. "Everything Is for Sale Now. Even Us." *The New York Times*, 24 Nov. 2018, https://www.nytimes.com/2018/11/24/opinion/sunday/gig-economy-self-promotion-anxiety.html.

WORTHAM, JENNA. "Pebble Raises $15 Million as Wave of Smart Watches Arrives." *The New York Times*, 16 May 2013, https://bits.blogs.nytimes.com/2013/05/16/pebble-raises-15-million-to-ready-itself-for-wave-of-smart watch-competitors/.

ZAVERI, MIHIR. "GoFundMe to Refund Border Wall Donations After Fund-Raiser Falls Short." *The New York Times*, 11 Jan. 2019, https://www.nytimes.com/2019/01/11/us/gofundme-border-wall-refund.html.

Index

This book is current up until the time of printing. For the most up-to-date reporting, visit www.nytimes.com.